You're Not Overdrawn

Just Underdeposited

(Blank Page)

YOU'RE NOT OVERDRAWN—

JUST UNDERDEPOSITED

How to Live With Class on Little Money
How to Manage Your Personal Finances

Beverlee Kelley

Griffin Publishing
Glendale, California

© 1992 by Beverlee Kelley

10   9   8   7   6   5   4   3   2

ISBN: 1-882-180-01-1

Griffin Publishing
544 West Colorado Street
Glendale, California

Manufactured in the United States of America.

CONTENTS

This book is dedicated to Lillian Nott,
a lady of great wit and charm,
who gave me the title.

WHO WILL GAIN BY READING THIS BOOK?

Today every check-writing billpayer is concerned with limited funds and is looking for a way to control personal finances. This book offers a simple solution to organizing and maintaining control, making it easier to "Live with Class" on little money. It doesn't matter how much money you have.

The author gives the reader new attitudes to use so as to feel more prosperous and less fearful about money. She discusses people's attitudes toward money and how they spend it. By identifying how others feel about money, the reader will gain insights into available options for enjoying his money.

One of the following profiles may fit your circumstances:

No Savings for Vacation

When you go on vacation, you still have to watch your pennies. You can't do all of the marvelous things that you would like to do. You want to enjoy the good life and be free of money worries for two weeks of the year. You need a plan.

You Don't Know How Much You Need

You are recently on your own—single, because of divorce or death. You have never had to deal with money totally on your own before. The CASH FLOW CHART will show you how much you will need to live on and how far your money will go. Investment advice is not part of this book, but no one should invest until he has the basics in order. The difference between what you will need to live on and what you have is what you can talk about to the investment planners.

More Wants than Cash

You are just starting out to build a career for yourself. For the first time, it looks as though you can begin to think about buying a home. You have lots of wants. More than you can do all at once. It is hard to be patient. This book offers you a plan. Put the COLORCODE CARD SYSTEM to work for you. See how you are gaining. Don't limit your dream, begin your plans!

You Need Cooperation from Your Spouse

You are a businessman and you understand money. Your wife doesn't understand why you have to cut back. You become frustrated because you don't like to be mean and ugly about it. How can you get her cooperation? Read this book and see if you agree with the ideas, and then ask her to read it so you can discuss how you feel. A third party can be helpful in getting the point across. This book can be that third party.

You Feel Stressed as Prices Rise

Higher prices are cutting back your buying power. Your friends seem to have more money than you do. You do not like to say you cannot afford all the things they suggest and you are embarrassed. Keeping up with the "Jones's" is getting you in trouble. You are losing your confidence in your own worth. The chapter on Prosperity is for you! Hold your head high and feel better!

Your Children Don't Understand

Your children think of you as a money machine. If they push the right button, you will give them what they want. They have no idea what they are doing to you financially. You resent their demands. They do not seem to appreciate you. How can you help them learn the value of money? Let them read this book. It can easily be understood by young people.

You Are Losing Hope

The years are going by too fast, and your hopes and aspirations are getting dim. You thought you would be able to do more than you have. You are losing your confidence. Your feeling of self-worth is slipping. If only you had more money, you could be closer to your dreams. Instead, you spend money on little luxuries because you can never afford the bigger ones anyway. You are giving up. The difference between what you have and what you want is too wide. It is like being on one side of the Grand Canyon without a bridge to get across to the other side. You need the prosperity attitudes given in this book because you are feeling sorry for yourself.

You Use Credit to Buy More Than You Can Afford

You are getting farther into debt each month. It is depressing to feel limited. How can you ever get ahead? The credit card information and the CASH FLOW CHART will give you incentive to make

some changes necessary to reverse your situation.
You can still live in a comfortable manner and not
overspend.

You Don't Like to Pay Bills

You worry every time you write a check because
you wonder if it will bounce. You suffer so much
that you put off paying bills. You are a good person,
but the telephone company is going to disconnect
your phone. You had the money, but you didn't sit
down and send out your check soon enough. "How
to Balance Your Check Book" and "Getting
Organized" will help you.

You Have a Good Income But You are Not Getting Ahead

You make good money, but you never have
anything to show for it. You wonder how other
people can do all the things they do. The chapters
"How to Spend Money for Nothing" and "Saving
Money by Spending It" and "Saving by Setting
Money Aside" are for you.

You Sacrifice for Your Children

You are parents of children who are out on their
own. They keep getting in trouble with their bills.
Just when you have gotten to the place where you
can spend for yourselves, the kids need help and
you have to put off your own enjoyment. The next
time they ask for a loan (which they may or may
not pay back), ask them to make out a COLORCODE
CARD SYSTEM and a CASH FLOW CHART before
you give them the money.

You Feel Like a Beggar When You Ask For Money

You have to ask your parents for money again.
Every time it gets harder. When you feel so small, it

is hard to be loving and kind to your parents because you feel guilty. How can you be considered independent if you have to crawl back and ask for help? You avoid writing or visiting the ones who care the most for you. Now you are more alone, but not more independent. You need a plan. Your parents will be impressed.

More Time Than Money

You have just retired. Your income is 50% of what it was last year. You don't know how long you will live or how high inflation will go. You would like to take trips and do other things you never had time for before, but now that you have the time, you have less money. What do you do? Go ahead and spend? The CASH FLOW CHART is really important to you. You can see if the interest on your capital and Social Security checks will be enough.

More Money Than Time

You have the money to pay bills, but your records are in such a mess that you really don't know what is what. You don't open your mail and you put your bills wherever you drop your things when you enter the house. Late payments are normal for you. There is no way for you to tell what has been paid so you put off paying anything. You will be able to save hundreds of dollars and develop a better credit rating when you use the Simple File System.

Chapter One

YOU'RE NOT OVERDRAWN
—JUST UNDERDEPOSITED

- Most people do not have a plan.
- Budgets are usually history.
- Increasing prices are scary.
- Prosperity is an attitude of Living with Class.

Suddenly everybody is talking about the economy—interest rates, investments, taxes, and equal pay for equal work. There is more sophistication about money than ever before. Yet, most people are financially embarrassed. They are not feeling comfortable about what they have because it is never enough, and they are not sure how to control what they have. Most do not know what the balance is in their checking account. Even bankers have confided in me that they could use the information I intend to share with you.

When I started talking about having a seminar on how to handle personal finances, I found out some truly amazing things. It was amazing to learn that a woman who has more money than I have ever had, has changed banks six times this past year because she couldn't figure out her statement. Then I was told that many people do the same thing—close their account when they don't know what amount is in it. I began to see that what was normally routine for me was not what other people did.

I would not feel comfortable writing a check if I though it would bounce. I am not saying those who close their accounts feel comfortable. In fact, they are uncomfortable or they would not be paying for new checks and troubling themselves with transferring their accounts. I am saying there is a way to know what you have in the bank and it is not always the same amount they tell you on the day you ask your bank—there may be some checks that have not cleared. Don't wait until you get your statement to find out your balance. Once a month is not enough. Each time you write a check you need to know your remaining balance.

I don't like budgets! A budget makes me feel guilty about how much things that I want or need cost. It is really a downer. Besides, most budgets are merely history and never get past what has been spent and on to the business of what you can do in the future. What I like is knowing I can pay for what I buy. What I like best is thinking about what I can do in the future that will make me feel freer to spend. After all, I deserve a good life and so do you!

I am fortunate because I like big numbers. Usually a big number is just a little number with a lot of zeros after it. I got used to big numbers when I became an insurance agent. It was exciting to talk about $100,000 policies to people who have never seen $100,000 in hand at one time. The most money we usually have at one time is the down payment for a car or a home.

If we are going to change our attitude about money, we need to think in terms of bigger numbers. Not just how to get through this month's bills, but how to plan for one, two or five years ahead. You have spent much more than $100,000 if you are over thirty years old. And you will be spending a bigger number in the next few years. You are very valuable! Wouldn't you like a financial statement that showed you are worth a lot right now?

Managing personal finances is exciting when you can see growth and improvement in your circumstances. The COLORCODE CARD SYSTEM is my answer to budgets. It goes beyond keeping track of history and into showing the progress you are making towards financial ease. The COLORCODE CARD SYSTEM is completely outlined in this book so you can design a plan for you that is comfortable. When you have a COLORCODE CARD SYSTEM in operation, you will be so beautifully organized. You will know what money you have to spend and will be making decisions more easily about how you want to spend it.

Price increases are scary. When we pay twice as much for the same item now as we paid just two or three years ago, we get a terrible feeling and the smile goes right off our faces. Going to the supermarket is not super any more, the prices just are. From what the newspapers and the TV tell us, it is going to be worse. No wonder everybody is talking about money! We begin to feel guilty for how much things cost and not having a bigger income. I cannot tell you in this book how to earn more money. This is not a book about investments or career improvements. I do plan, however, to cover the ways to handle the income you have and how to avoid the "guilties".

First, let's look at interest rates. To give you an idea of the effect of interest rates upon your future accummulated savings, we will use a simplified version of the Rule of 72. Though not exact, the answer comes close. Take the current rate of interest and divide into 72. For example: if the rate is 10% per year—dividing 10 into 72 gives us 7.2 and that answer is the number of years (should the rate of interest stay the same) that your money will be worth 200% of what it is now. In other words, if you save $1.00 now it will be $2.00 in 7.2 years. Interesting isn't it? 10% is more than most savings accounts earn. Below are some other figures.

Rate of Interest	Years Until $ Value is 200%
10%	7
9%	8
8%	9
7%	10
6%	12

Unfortunately, we pay income tax on most interest bearing accounts, so if we are in the 15% tax bracket, we need to earn 12% to clear 10%. The individual in the 31% tax bracket has to earn 14.5% interest on their capital to clear 10% as available income. Those savings that are tax free (IRA's etc.) while accummulating are getting more preferable all the time.

Hopefully all the above information will not make you want to go camping for the rest of your life. The point is that we can be more aware of what is happening, so we don't become victims of our own lack of understanding.

Remember this:

You are not responsible for what
things cost, only for how to
handle what it costs.

Planning is your protection. Planning to limit your family is a good investment. The cost of raising a child to age eighteen is around $150,000 for a first child and not much less for additional children. That does not include piano lessons and sports activities. Even after a child becomes an adult, you always seem to have more money than they do (in their eyes) and they come back to help you spend it.

Why should you feel guilty for what things cost? That kind of guilt is futile and ridiculous. It reminds me of when I first started playing bridge. Whenever my partner had a strong hand and opened the bid, and I had a poor hand with hardly enough points to answer, I would feel guilty. Silly me! Where do you think the extra points in my partner's hand came from? The other hands, of course. I was not responsible for what cards I was dealt, only for what I did with them. If you feel you are responsible for the deal, then I for one don't want to play with a cheat. So don't take on the guilt of what things cost. Only concern yourself with how you spend your money.

Personal attention to money management is a big void in most people's thinking. Ask someone how long they will live, and it is forever. Ask how long they will be able to work and they are never going to retire. Ask how much they are saving for the time between jobs, or when they are ill or too old to work, and they pretend to know the answer to how to avoid life's problems. The truth is that you will never meet a widow who thought her husband had too much life insurance. This book is not to sell you insurance. It is designed to give you some new attitudes about money; something to think about now, while you have options.

Another thing I don't like is surprises. Just when you think you are cutting the stack of bills down, BOOM! the auto insurance is due. It was kind of in the back of your mind, but you kept hoping it wouldn't happen. I will tell you my method for anticipating the surprise bills when we discuss the COLORCODE CARD SYSTEM and CASH FLOW CHART.

Since I am not perfect about being organized and I don't expect you to be, I have a system that requires attention only on the day you receive your income. It is only fun to pay bills when there is something to pay them with, so put all your bills in one place until the next batch of money comes in. DON'T WORRY, BE HAPPY—JUST DON'T SPEND ANY MONEY YOU DON'T HAVE!

You have to know what you are doing in order to do it right. For example, there was the person who could not seem to pay the right amount to the electric company each month. The electric company would receive an amount less than the bill one month and receive an amount more than the bill another month. After many calls back and forth, the person at the electric company found the answer to the riddle and said, "Please look at your bill. Do you see the amount in the lower right hand corner? That is the amount to write the check for—the number you have been using is the date." Ridiculous? Maybe. We have to pay attention to what we look at, so we really see what is there.

Of course the electric company could learn a lesson from the experience also. Perhaps the style of the form needs to be changed. All bills these days have more information than people use. There is a lot of helpful information and we will be using some of that information in our evaluations, but you have to pay attention in order to use the information to your advantage.

If you don't see well you are more likely to make mistakes in your checkbook, avoid doing your bookkeeping and getting nervous when you have to do paperwork. When I started wearing glasses all of the time, I noticed that I was much more calm about detail work and relieved to be able to see more clearly. Your eyes will like the system I am going to tell you about, because you can use felt tip pens and write as large as you like.

The real value of this book is the thoughts about prosperity. Prosperity is the attitude of success. "Living with Class" even on little money is a creative experience. Broke, but never poor may be where you are now. Why not feel prosperous? No matter what your income, there are ways to enjoy either a good feeling, or suffer a poor one, about what you have.

Even a millionaire can feel poor. The uncle of a friend of mine had a million dollars before the market crash of the twenties. After the crash, he was worth half a million. Half a million dollars in 1930 was a real fortune! According to my friend's Aunt Cookie, he was so upset, so depressed, he died. (Your name can be Cookie and still command respect if you are married to a millionaire.) I choose to feel prosperous.

I do not suffer well. Some people are good at it. Like the man who worked in a factory. When the noon whistle blew, he would take his brown paper bag to the same place every day. And every day he would take out his peanut butter sandwich, open it up, growl angry words and then throw it away. There was another man who saw this happening every day and wanted to be helpful. He said to the first man, "If you don't like peanut butter, why don't you tell your wife?" To which the first man replied, "You leave my wife out of this. I make my own lunch!" He is a suffering person who prefers his problem to the solution. He doesn't mind imposing his suffering upon others, either. UGH!

"What do you have in your lunch?"
"Peanut butter sandwiches. *@*!"
"If you don't like peanut butter, why don't you tell your wife?"
"You leave my wife out of this. I make my own lunch!"

Any immature person can complain. Most complainers think that if they can tell you what is wrong (with the economy or any other subject) that makes them an authority. Wrong. They are only experts in complaining. Mature persons know they don't know everything, don't pretend to know everything, and make the best of what they do understand. They are more inclined to sleep well, keep their friends, and they can laugh at themselves for the mistakes they make.

The way to feel prosperous is to appreciate what we have and to keep a happy attitude.

SUMMARY

1. Most people do not have a plan for how to spend.

2. Budgets are usually only a history of what has been spent. You need something better than a budget.

3. Increasing prices are scary. We will have less buying power in the future unless we save money now, as shown by the Rule of 72.

4. Taking responsibility for how we spend does not have to be a depressing chore.

5. Prosperity is an attitude of Living with Class, even if you have little money.

Chapter Two

HOW TO SPEND MONEY FOR NOTHING

- It is easy to spend money.
- Ways to spend for no value.
- Anticipating possible problems saves money.

We can easily spend money for nothing unless we are aware of what we are doing and prevent it from happening. Preventive action such as checking your car to see that it has enough gasoline, enough fluid in the radiator, fluid in the transmission and steering mechanism, air in the tires, and belts in good condition, saves BIG money.

I am fortunate to have mechanics at the gas station near my home who help me avoid costly expenses by suggesting preventative maintenance such as new fan belts and hoses before they break. What friends they are! Negative people might say that they are making more money by telling me to spend for such things. Sure, it increases their income, but it saves me time and money, and I do not resent other's gain when it is my gain also.

The best way to throw away money is to neglect your car. One long slow line of traffic with no way to escape and an overheated car, and you need $500.00

worth of repairs, plus your car is never the same. I saw it happen to a lady right in front of me while we were stuck in line while a construction job held up traffic. How sad.

Sometimes if we laugh at the extremes, we see related messages more clearly. Here is a list of ways to spend money for nothing. I won't tell you which ones I have observed in others and which ones I have done myself. I don't mind your knowing how I think, but I would rather you didn't remember me for my mistakes.

- Get a traffic ticket. Not only will you give the municipal clerk money, but your auto insurance will go up for three years, and credit checks on your character will go down. (Unreliable, impulsive, foolish, etc.) It pays to go to traffic school, if you have that option.
- Leave your car in a No Parking zone. This doesn't raise your insurance, but it does throw money away. If you don't pay the ticket, you have a warrant out for your arrest. That means that if you are stopped by a policeman for anything such as jaywalking, they do a check and off you go to jail immediately. Sometimes they come looking for you. (The neighbors are apt to think you are guilty of much more than a parking ticket.)
- Pay your bills after the due date. The late charge can be as much as $1.50 or higher for a $10.00 payment. That is 15% which adds up to 18% per year. Ouch!
- Throw away receipts so that you cannot take back unwanted purchases. If

something doesn't fit or is tacky, give it to the thrift shop. The write-off on your income tax is all you can recover. Oh, yes, be sure to get a receipt from the thrift shop.

- Pay deposits that you forfeit. Deposits are not always refundable. Deposits are called earnest money to show intent to purchase. That is why they are not always refundable.
- Rent a car that sits in the parking lot all day. A taxi could be a better bargain.
- When you travel get the most expensive accommodations and then only sleep in them. Or the other extreme—get a special low price because the hotel is located out of the district you are going to and spend the difference on transportation and time.
- Buy an item of clothing that you have to use only once.

"How do you like my witch costume? I paid $75.00 for it!"
"Do you play witch very often?"

- Keep the lights on, the heat up, or the air conditioning on and the TV going when nobody cares.

- Cook more than you eat—order more than you need—buy perishables in larger quantities than you use.
- Own equipment you seldom use. It can go out of style or deteriorate. Renting ski equipment is an example of an alternative.
- Buy the most expensive item when a lesser priced item would do the trick, like an expensive camera when the purpose is to take snapshots. What do you need with a zoom lens?
- Subscribe to magazines you don't read. They add clutter and the guilties. Both are detrimental to your prosperity and health. Use your local library and get your use out of the tax money you contribute.

"Why can't you put your car in the garage?"

"Because George has all his fishing gear, ski equipment, backpacking gear and golf clubs in there."

"I don't remember him talking about those things."

"Oh, he doesn't do them, he just buys the stuff!"

- Let a check bounce. You get a bank charge, plus embarrassment! You know you don't belong in jail. That is where they send people who write bad checks.
- Get a cigarette burn in your couch right where it shows.
- Live in a larger house than you need. This is debatable. It depends upon whether you own your home and if it is increasing in value, how long you have owned it and what it would cost to buy a smaller one. Likely as not your taxes may go up, the interest rate on a new loan would be higher and the cost of moving is too high. If you are renting perhaps you should own a home.
- Sell your house a few months before you are 55 and throw away the option of getting a tax write-off on your capital gains.

I think you have the idea now about how to throw away money. You can add to the list from your own experiences and observations. If you want to throw away money, it is more fun to go to Las Vegas.

I am not a fortuneteller, thank goodness. I would find life a bore if I thought what was going to happen was all worked out. At the same time, there is a certain number of things I can predict with clarity: things like Christmas, birthdays, taxes, and such. Every one of those things costs money. The COLORCODE CARD SYSTEM puts all those items into the system ahead of need. If I wait until the last minute to shop or to set aside cash to handle them, it costs me more money. The gift purchased at the last minute becomes more expensive and, if I must borrow money to pay taxes, I pay interest.

"Could you wrap it as a gift?"
"You look like you are going to a wedding."
"I am. That's why I need the gift."

Anticipating future needs and preparing for them relieves you of much stress. Less stress means better health. Poor health can cost lots and lots of money! Avoid the risk.

SUMMARY

1. It is easy to spend money for nothing.

2. Any time we spend money we don't have to, and that money is spent for something that gives us no value, we have spent money for nothing.

3. Anticipating possible repairs helps avoid spending for bigger problems.

4. The COLORCODE CARD SYSTEM helps us think in terms of the future and how to anticipate what is needed.

Chapter Three

FEELINGS WE HAVE ABOUT MONEY

- How much money we have determines how we feel.
- Money is only important when we feel limited.
- Spending means giving away power.
- Money gives us choices.

I feel great when I have money in my bank account, cash in my wallet, and all the bills are paid. I feel rotten when I am looking for enough money to go around, have to say "No" to something I want, and my checkbook is down to zero. It is hard for me to be motivated to work harder when I am edgy. Some folks are more ambitious when they are in need and lazy when they are comfortable. Not me! I really get excited about doing productive things when I am happy and my world is in order.

Since I don't like feeling guilty about not making enough money, I try to avoid incurring expenses that are a burden. Later on, I will share with you my list of questions to ask yourself before making a purchase. It helps to control spending for things that are not important to you and save you from adding expenses you don't need.

Surplus cash is a super luxury. What a nice dream. Wouldn't it be great to have the feeling that we could spend without caring about the cost? Wow! The truth is money is only important to you if you don't have enough or feel that you don't have enough. To me, materialistic people are the ones obsessed with the cost of things and greedily trying to acquire as many show-off luxuries as possible. To enjoy what you have, to care for it, and to share it with others is not being materialistic.

Recently, I saw a four-year-old boy going along the main street of a resort area driving a motorized car that was just the right size for him. Imagine, a four-year-old with an expensive motorized vehicle on the sidewalk? Then I realized that he is not going to grow up thinking in limited ways about how to enjoy life. If that toy represents a reservoir of wealth, then there are other good things to come. Is there any good reason why he should not enjoy the toy? Is there any good reason why his parents or (more likely) his grandparents should not have the joy of giving him such a toy? I think not. MONEY IS ONLY IMPORTANT IF YOU THINK YOU DON'T HAVE ENOUGH. (To the same degree that health becomes important when you are sick.)

"Money is only important to you
if you don't have enough."

Another way we show how we care too much about money is the way we treat everything we have as if it is our last time to own such a nice object. If owning a silver tea service is a heavy responsibility to you—you hide it from burglars, worry about it being tarnished, won't let your friend wash it for you after a party for fear that it will get damaged—then I would say you are working for the tea service and it is not serving your needs. Uptight attitudes about possessions are difficult. Caring for things because they are lovely and appreciated does not have to become an obsession.

Every time you spend money, you are giving away power. If what you give your money for brings you more power, you win; if you spend for something that weakens your position, you lose. Let me explain.

In order to be able to earn income, you need to be healthy. Therefore, money spent on keeping healthy such as nourishing food, a comfortable home environment, clothing that supports a good self-image, and basic necessities that give you a feeling of wellness and prosperity, is money well spent.

Buying food that is not an aid to good health is giving away your power. The cost of empty calorie junk food is so destructive, it is sometimes more expensive than nutritious food. The only way to avoid these temptations is not to buy them in the first place.

The same goes for the money you spend on clothes. A few good quality items in your wardrobe will do a lot more for you than lots of faddish or poor quality clothes. Some people spend a lot of money to look awful. Clear out the unflattering things you have because they take away from your power to express an attractive self.

The exception to the quality idea is when you are buying clothes for children. They get such tough wear and tear, and those little people get to be bigger people so fast. Brothers and sisters really don't like hand-me-downs.

In order to be able to earn income, you may need to spend money in order to make money. Promoting and advertising your product or services is necessary to create more income and to continue to generate the income you now have. Even the I.R.S. agrees with this and gives you the option of deducting such costs.

In order to be able to earn income, you may need to spend money for supplies or tools. The right tool can be the difference in how much you can earn. My laser printer cost a lot of money, but the first year it generated income that was greater than the cost. Without that printer, I could not have been able to offer a complete service to my clients. That printer gave me power equal to more than the cost. So spending money did not lessen my power, but increased it.

In order to be able to earn income, you may need to spend money for education. A course or obtaining a degree which gives you a job skill or improves a job skill can give you more power and is money well spent.

It is OK to spend money on friends. Friends are important to your power. They enhance your circle of influence. Your connections can be beneficial to your earning capacity. Consider friends as an investment. They bring you pleasure, help you find a job, bring you business contacts, share their knowledge, and save you money. You can be a real asset to them for all the same reasons. A support network of friends is stimulating and satisfying. You learn so much from people with whom you develop an open and sharing relationship.

You feel big when you have options and can make wise choices. You feel small when you have little power.

As George Bernard Shaw said, "The lack of money is the root of all evil." Most arguments about money are concerned with the limitations of money, not the abundance of it. How we feel about money reflects our attitude toward life in general. If we feel inadequate and unable to cope or are depressed, it is often related to our sense of self-worth. We equate self-worth with what we have, how much we make, and what hope we have of getting what we want. I am not saying that is right or wrong, it just is.

You are a very valuable person. Multiply the amount of money you earn in one year by the number of years you have before reaching 65 and you see you are very valuable.

What makes one person feel secure is more or less what makes another person feel secure. Remember the husband of Aunt Cookie? The amount is not as important as the feelings of restriction, limitation, or abundance. Even people who do not handle their own money are influenced. Children and spouses who do not pay bills receive feelings of generosity or miserliness from those who handle money. Having good relationships with others is dependent upon a feeling of giving and caring.

The misers have a hard time being forgiving persons because they are not generous in anything they do. Because they are worriers, they are always looking for the flaw, the trap, and where they might be a victim They are not trusting, so it becomes a self-fulfilling prophecy. They get what they are looking for. We have a hard time trusting a miser, because we figure they are seeking only their own good, not ours, and therefore cannot find a common good for both of us. And because they worry and call every event a crisis, we tune them out even if they have a point.

So health, wealth, good relationships and self-expression are interdependent, and all must be of a prosperous attitude for you to be successful.

Success is equated with the feeling of power to make choices that are beneficial to you. The opposite is the person who feels trapped and a victim of circumstances. Money gives you choices. When you spend money, be sure it brings you a feeling of power.

Understanding success comes from being happy for others who are successful. What can you learn from successful people? What gave them the feeling of confidence? To say that some folks are too rich is like saying, "I don't understand wealth." The successful ones are the ones who make opportunities for others, not just for themselves.

An unsuccessful business cannot create jobs, cannot invest, cannot build, cannot expand. A successful business is one that spreads the wealth by investing in people and materials. A successful person invests and spreads the wealth through capitalizing on other people's ventures. No one is collecting dollars and keeping them idle. The power of the dollar is given to many people as it passes through different hands. One dollar in your wallet now has also been one dollar in someone else's pocket. The circulation of money is worth more than the dollar itself.

Money in the bank is not idle either. Until you call for your money by writing a check, that money is in circulation.

By now, you have probably noticed the word power, as referred to here, is not a negative word as in power to hurt.

This book is concerned with developing a plan of control for expanding your self-worth, so that you will have a greater respect for the power of your money and what you can do with it. We are talking about tools for controlling your personal income so that you can enjoy what you do with it. If you have a feeling of prosperity now, you can gain a feeling of greater efficiency using the organizational information. If you are in debt and would sincerely like to get ahead of your bills, the attitudes of prosperity will help you change your pattern of spending without feeling like a miser.

An idea becomes your idea when you develop a positive attitude about it. Develop a prosperous attitude if you want to live more fully.

SUMMARY

1. How much money we have to spend determines how comfortable we feel about our obligations.

2. Money is only important to you when you think you don't have enough.

3. Spending money is giving away power unless what we spend it for brings us power.

4. It is important to be able to spend money on yourself.

5. Success is equated with being able to make choices; lack of success with having limitations.

6. Successful relationships with others are dependent upon having a generous attitude.

7. Understanding success comes from being happy for the success of others as well as yourself.

8. The purpose of having a plan is so you can enjoy what you do with your money.

Chapter Four

HOW TO AVOID THE FINANCIAL "GUILTIES"

- Game-playing when we are financially embarrassed.
- Everybody is doing the best he can or he would do better.
- Seven steps for avoiding the "guilties".

Can you look your landlord in the eye? Do you get nervous when you open your mail? Are you afraid to answer the phone? Are you and your bank good friends? I hope you are laughing, not cringing when I mention the above. All of us have had times when we have been financially embarrassed. Even the most wealthy group of professionals, doctors, had times during med school and when starting their practice when they were very broke. Maybe that is why they become investors—they never want to repeat the experience.

Even wealthy people who are invested to the hilt have times when their cash flow is down, and they must postpone an expense. Ask their newspaper boy how many times he has had to go back for his money. My former landlord, who owns four buildings, each of which is worth several million dollars, had to have my rent money before he could pay the mortgage payment. I tell you this so you don't feel alone.

What happens when a person feels guilty about not having enough money? They either take a defensive posture or an offensive one. They start playing games. The defensive action is to avoid the problem, blame it on the economy, and try to find a diversion like going out and partying, which makes everything worse. The offensive action is to deny the situation, act as if they were overcharged or taken advantage of, and try to make it someone else's problem. Both extremes are uncomfortable to live with.

The mental anguish of being broke leads us to a series of events that is a downward spiral. For instance, you may be very young and earning little, yet you need a car. You may have enough for a down payment, but you hesitate to even look for one, because you don't think anyone in his right mind would lend you the money. Then you read the ads, hoping to find a car for sale by owner. You end up buying a car from someone who also is feeling guilty. He knows he hasn't taken care of the car he is selling you, that it has mechanical problems, and he is so glad to get rid of it he will "let" you buy it and never ask about your credit rating. You end up with more expense and the problem of not having what you need—a car in good working order! Plus now you are guilty of having been taken advantage of. In other words, when we are in a weak position mentally, we seem to draw problems to ourselves. How sad it is that those people who do not make much money often have to pay more for less.

There is a premise I use which makes me feel better. It makes my relationships with other people go much smoother. I don't get my feelings hurt unnecessarily. I forgive other people for what they do more readily, and it protects me from becoming a self-righteous person. The premise is:

Everybody is doing the best they can or they would do better!

This applies to me, too. I have done the best I could do under the circumstances of how I felt, the knowledge I have had at the time, the pressures of other things that were happening in my life, what I thought was important, what I wanted to happen, how I felt about the people I was dealing with, and my fears of what might happen, or the hope of what could happen—all the intangibles which are conscious, or unconscious, and often forgotten after the event. It feels so good to be a winner! It feels so much nicer to be free of heavy burdens. It is so pleasing to please others when it flows. Therefore, I forgive myself for what I cannot erase. Now, I can make a decision to act that does not come from fear. The decision comes from WHAT IS GOOD FOR ME— AND FEELS RIGHT, which includes what feels good for others as well.

The premise EVERYBODY IS DOING THE BEST THEY CAN OR THEY WOULD DO BETTER! may or may not be true, but it makes life so much less stressful and I like the results when I think this way. Try it.

If you happen to be one of the many people who have always spent whatever they have to spend, because they felt times were always getting better, (there are lots of paychecks ahead and, besides, you will be earning more later) you are not alone. Such faith! I would not want to dampen your spirit. You may be right! Your belief that there will be more is the same spirit that will get you more. Why not enjoy and live for today?

But, do you know that tomorrow becomes today and that you are betting on the future? To ignore preparing for a more prosperous tomorrow is to take away some of tomorrow's freedoms. Inflation does two things to this attitude: one, it gives you the awareness that you have fewer options when your money purchases less than before and, two, it gives you the excuse to go ahead and spend as before, because what you buy now costs less than what you would have to pay later.

Somewhere there has to be balance. The person who has cash in large amounts can pay less than the person who has little cash and must pay full price and finance costs or let the opportunity go by. The people without cash feel guilty for paying more, and kick themselves for not having saved. The IF's get to them: "IF I had the down payment, I could be paying myself instead of the landlord." What are you afraid of? How much would it hurt to not be a spender? What will people think of you, IF you don't have a new outfit for the party? What would people think IF you took the bus, instead of having a second car? Some people are afraid that if they don't spend money, they will become lazy about earning a living and will lose their motivation for "getting ahead." Some wives have the attitude that IF they don't spend, their husbands will level off and be satisfied. They won't want to try for the promotion, or the bigger deal, or the additional sale. We create our own monsters, our own ulcers, our own fears.

Perhaps what we are most afraid of is that we are going to be dull, old-acting, miserly grouches, if we slow down our spending. We don't want to be a killjoy. Perhaps we have noticed that the financial managers in companies and organizations are the least liked. They are avoided because they ask the meaningful question, "Is this expense necessary?" But, there are creative minded financial people, as well as conservative sales managers. Corporations and individuals gain from having a perspective which includes both aspects for balance.

You as an individual, need to have both a practical side and a creative side. In a partnership, in a man/woman relationship, each needs to be understanding of both aspects to enjoy harmony. If one member of a partnership is always taking the role of being careful and the other the role of the spender, there is division and mistrust develops. I pity the wife who hides her shopping splurge in the back of the closet, or the husband who doesn't mention the purchase of a new tool or sports equipment. New purchases are more enjoyable if there is joy in sharing the acquisition. Anticipation of planning for a new item can be part of the joy in having "a new toy." Ebb and flow are natural elements of life, processes rather than competing forces. Sometimes you can afford to spend and sometimes you can't.

Where there are children involved, both aspects need to be taught and those ideas discussed as part of daily living. Children given reasonable explanations and the opportunity to participate in decision-making are better prepared for the bigger responsibilities of their future. Too many times there is a race to see who can get their share first, whine the most, demand the most, before the supply is exhausted. This comes from a fear of limitation and an atmosphere of unfairness. Appreciation for what we have needs to be expressed.

Some people are caught up in their own ambition for improving their lot in life and strive so hard to pretend that they are already in the next higher place, that they never can afford what they do. Please do picture yourself making progress. Please do know you deserve to be successful. Please do not lose the light at the end of the tunnel. You will get there faster if you go more slowly.

Right <Guilt Feelings> Wrong
Beginning to Feel Guilty is Half Way
Between Feeling Right or Wrong.

When you feel uncomfortable, it is time to learn something or take action which you know will make you more comfortable. Listen to your body, mind, and emotions. They are biofeedback in regard to your relationships with others and yourself. If you feel sleepy and you insist upon doing what you are doing, you are going against a body need. Of course, you can't stop driving in the middle of the fast lane and take a snooze. Usually you have gradual warnings before you have a problem. So it is with feeling guilty about not having enough money, or being behind in paying your bills. The feeling of guilt can be an indicator of being in the halfway place between doing something wrong for you and getting to the place where you are satisfied with your actions.

The hardest part of growing is the state of confusion before the awakening (clarity). If you back off and avoid the experience, you have limited your growth for now and possibly forever. I would rather have a new level of understanding and have new problems (like what to do with all my money) than to be like the man with the peanut butter sandwich. How about you?

The answer to "How to Avoid the Financial 'Guilties' is in this chapter. I will simplify the main points here:

1. Forgive yourself. Everybody is doing his best and so are you.

2. Evaluate. What have you learned? What is the situation? What caused it?

3. Organize. See where you are and prepare for a new start.

4. Look at your options. Think about solutions (robbing a bank is out of bounds), list them, and pick the ones you want to try that feel

comfortable or are the most possible to live with.

5. Develop a plan. Put your plan on paper. You may want to use my plan, THE COLORCODE CARD SYSTEM, as suggested later in this book.

6. Take action. Plans are only good if you use them.

7. Re-evaluate. If your plan is not working, you may have to start with number 1 again.

You are the authority for what works best for you. You may create a plan that is better than my plan. So do it. Be proud of yourself!

CAUTION! New habits are not easy to keep. Do not give up if you give a lot of energy to the ideas in this book and then let down. You are not limited to how many times you can begin. JUST READ THIS BOOK AGAIN AND START OVER.

SUMMARY

1. All of us have been financially embarrassed at some time.

2. Defensive or offensive postures lead to game-playing and are uncomfortable.

3. Everybody is doing the best they can or they would do better. That includes you. Forgive yourself!

4. Think about what it is that frightens you. Name it.

5. Balance between being practical and having creative enjoyment is possible within the same person and is needed in partnerships.

6. You become more successful, faster, if you go more slowly.

7. If you are uncomfortable, it is time to learn something. Learn the lesson, rather than repeat it.

8. Use the seven steps to take to avoid the "guilties".

Chapter Five

LIVING WITH CLASS—PROSPERITY

- Decide to be prosperous.
- Quit feeling sorry for yourself.
- Eight ways to say "No" by creating options.

Have you decided to be prosperous or are you satisfied with just survival? Nothing is wrong with just surviving if you are happy. In fact, some people with handicaps or burdens of responsibility who survive in an honest effort, are to be commended. But, most of us want more than survival. To be prosperous, one must make a decision.

There is something to the statement that when you do not make a decision, you have already made a decision not to make one. If you are not a decision-maker, then you had better stay in the low income bracket where the basic decision is whether to eat or not. Choice of menu may be all you can handle. I have seen some who have difficulty with that.

Money gives you choices. When you have adequate money, you can order the least expensive item on the menu because you want it and not because it is the only thing you can afford. Having money does not mean you have to spend the total amount available.

"Do you want thousand island,
bleu cheese or oil and vinegar
dressing?"
"I can't make up my mind. Just give
me the house dressing."

Everybody has money to spend. Even poor people have some money to spend. Even poor people spend some money foolishly. The quality of your life will improve if the ways you spend money are for the best use of it. This takes good decision-making.

Few people have large amounts of cash on hand. All but the eccentric folk invest surplus cash, so even the wealthy do not carry much cash. Howard Hughes never carried any money on his person. Do not feel bad if you do not have much money in your wallet right this minute. You are smart not to carry cash if you would spend it unwisely. On the other hand, having a $100.00 bill in your wallet encourages a prosperous attitude.

A prosperous attitude is the difference between living with class and being a poor-me type of person. Feeling sorry for yourself is the most demeaning thing you can do to yourself. As I read the articles about people who have lived a long life and their comments about how they did it, they usually show an attitude which reflects no regrets for what might have been. They have accepted their circumstances in a way that shows they did the best they could and they know it.

Few of them have been wealthy, yet they did not feel sorry for themselves.

Living with class is a skill. How we talk about our circumstances to others has a lot to do with how people think we feel. If we blame others for the lack of substance in our life, we are belittling ourselves for not having earned the regard, support, and cooperation of other people. To stay in a situation that never heals is to say we have accepted that we do not deserve better.

There are many distractions from your goal of being prosperous. If you do not have a plan, you will be torn each time someone asks you to do something that is tempting and delays saving for your personal goal. At the same time, you want to avoid projecting a lack of prosperity.

Saying "I can't afford it" is programming yourself for being unsuccessful. To avoid the distraction, and to feel good about how we turn away an opportunity to spend money, we need to orient ourselves to the goal we have chosen for our plan. At the same time, we want to save face and speak in such a way as to be gracious. What we don't need is negative feedback but respect for our values.

Here are creative responses you can give. If someone asks you to go to Mexico, which is very nice of them to ask, and you want to refuse, you might try saying:

- "Thank you for asking me. (Always say thank you first so you do not give the impression you don't want to be with them. It is what they are offering you are refusing, not them.) I am pleased you want me to go with you. However, I am saving for (a new car) and I am eager to put aside as much as possible." (Fill in the parentheses with your desired goal.)

- "Thank you for asking me. There is something I want to do that weekend but I hope you have a good time."
- "Sounds like fun, but how about fixing the backyard instead, so we can give a party?"
- "Thank you for asking me. I would love to go when I get my project done, which should be in June." (Studying for an exam, remodeling the house, refinishing the furniture, etc.)
- "Thank you for asking me. I really enjoy going to the beach closer to home. Do you want to go with me? We can plan to bicycle along the boardwalk and get some exercise."
- "Thank you for asking me. I am busy. There is a concert at the college that weekend and I want to attend."
- "Thank you for asking me. Friends of mine have offered their cabin in the mountains. Would you like to go there?"
- "Let's stay home and invite some friends over for a barbecue. There are some people we have been meaning to entertain."

The main idea is to create options for yourself that avoid unnecessary expenditures. Options that are interesting and satisfying, yet do not take away from your goal of directing money elsewhere. Certainly there are benefits to having a remodeled house or a well-kept backyard that last longer than a weekend in Mexico. There are times to be free and to take a vacation without a care... IF IT IS PART OF YOUR PLAN.

Taking care of what you have gives you a more prosperous attitude as well as a prosperous appearance to your environment. Waxing and polishing your car is a good investment of your time. You will be more likely to be satisfied with it and keep it longer, which can save you money, maybe as much as a year's worth of car payments.

You feel more prosperous when you have staples on hand such as paper goods, shampoo, canned goods, even extra hosiery. Having an abundance of what you need is a good feeling as well as a convenience. If you have food items in the house and company comes, you can be the gracious host without a hassle. Your company feels less as if they are imposing if you can do this easily. It saves going out to eat, which gets expensive.

Parent in shower:
"Get some money out of my wallet and go to the store for some shampoo—quick!"

Having a prosperous attitude includes expressing gratitude for what you have, and building on your strengths rather than on your weaknesses. Spend some time alone to reflect upon your good fortune. Daydreaming is not only relaxing, but necessary to let new ideas come to us and for reflection of the past for new understanding.

Many people who work and live with people around them all the time seldom have a chance to be lazy. I once had a job that required forty-five minutes driving time on the freeway to get to the office. My acquaintances would say, "Oh, don't you hate that drive?" No. It was my time to be alone. I would turn off the radio so I would not be distracted.

If you are not used to being alone, you may find it difficult at first, but you can get hooked on it. Believe me, it is a luxury. Takes all the pressure off. It is beneficial to your mental health and has the added advantage of not costing money.

Once you have taken time to think about the positive things in your life, and have expressed your positive thoughts with others, they will see you are handling your problems in a mature manner and give you a more supportive attitude. Let people see you are a winner. Winners are people who make the effort to solve their problems—not just complain.

Take time to listen to your family and friends. Enjoy a sunset. There will never be another one just like the one you are seeing. Smell the flowers. A person I know said he made a point of taking just one of his children at a time out to dinner so they could express themselves more freely. It was a special time together without interruptions from other family members. The child felt he had Dad's full attention and would share his concerns. Dad learned what was going on in his child's world and could give guidance and encouragement. What a precious time to remember. Everyone needs an audience. "The future is not as scary if you talk it over with Dad first." Those talks were the arena for plans regarding what to do next week, far off plans for careers and ways to grow.

The dinner table at home can be a trying time for children as well as their parents. Since it is the only time when some families are together, it often takes on the atmosphere of being in court. Being judged, put on the spot in front of others who will use personal information as a weapon, does not feel good. Table manners include not just how we handle food but also how we handle conversation and personal relationships. The family dinner table is also the place where attitudes about money are taught. Attitudes of lack or prosperity. Attitudes about work and rewards, satisfaction of accomplishments, and solutions to problems, plans and sharing. Perhaps the ingredient missing at most dinner tables is light-hearted humor—the overview of not taking everything literally and being too serious. Living with class includes learning to laugh at one's self.

Plans are dreams until you make them real. Until you can see in your mind what you are trying to do, you will have a difficult time going in the direction that brings you good results. Outlining what needs to be done in order to get to your dream makes it possible to see that the dream can be real. As you experience each step along the way, you gain momentum and the way gets easier.

Right now, make a list of what you need to do to feel more prosperous. Get out of debt, have more money in the bank (state an amount), plan a vacation, decide on a major purchase (name it), enroll in special courses that would increase your earning capacity, improve your appearance (list what you want to do), live in a different area, drive a better car, or fix up the house. Whatever you want you can dream about. Pick one you can do right away; the one that perks up your attitude, one that will improve your condition.

When selecting this first plan, be careful not to overload your debt situation. For instance, you may want a new car. Yet you have credit cards that have been used up to the limit. Better to postpone adding a financial burden to an already stretched-to-the-limit monthly expense total. Perhaps the first part of your big plan is to take a course that will increase your earning capacity. Or maybe improving your appearance is the most motivating thing you can do to feel more prosperous.

Here is a list of steps to take to make your dream come true:

1. In one simple sentence, state what you want.

2. List everything you can think of that will bring you closer to, or complete, your desired solution. Example: go shopping and compare prices, decide what you need, see what you have, etc.

3. Select what is the most possible and the most important to you and reorganize your list (#2) in order of priority.

4. Set a time limit and deadline for achieving your goal.

5. Within that time limit (#4), divide the time into units. For instance, you want a more attractive appearance which includes a new wardrobe, a better hair style, and having a manicure done professionally. Your deadline is six months. Decide what you will

buy and what you will have done in the first month and each of the other months to arrive at your goal. If weight loss is involved then obviously you would put major clothing purchases nearer the end of your time limit so that you fit into your new wardrobe.

6. Give yourself a reward for each level of your plan so you feel good about the effort you are making. Deny yourself something you like if you don't live up to your commitment. List these in your plan.

7. Re-evaluate at each level and see if you have a plan that works. You may have to start over.

Be realistic about what you can accomplish. A plan that is too difficult is apt to fail. Be successful and like yourself better, not the reverse!

To have a prosperous attitude means to think in a positive way. If there are people in your life who are negative and try to distract you from what you know is good for you, then just smile at them and do not share your plan with them. What they don't know, they can't fight. Though it can be unimportant to them, it can be VERY important to you. You deserve to feel prosperous.

SUMMARY

1. Have you decided to be prosperous?

2. Money gives you choices.

3. Do you feel sorry for yourself?

4. Blaming others is not going to solve the problem.

5. Handle distractions with the eight ways to say "No" without saying, "I can't afford it."

6. Create options that are inexpensive.

7. When you have what you need, you feel prosperous.

8. Gratitude for what you have is the first step to feeling prosperous.

9. Taking time to be alone is important so you can plan.

10. Making a plan for what you want is a good way to get ahead.

Chapter Six

GETTING ORGANIZED

- It takes time to be disorganized.
- When you need legal advice, go to a professional.
- The supplies you will need

It takes time to be disorganized. You thought it took time to become organized and have put it off for that reason. Excuses, excuses. How many times have you searched for a piece of paper and looked everywhere before you found it? Looked in pockets, purses, dresser drawers, on desk counter tops, by the phone, in the car, in your briefcase, in the pile of mail and asked others to do the same? It might spoil your fun if there was only one place to look, but on the other hand, the priority is to have the piece of paper, not the game of trying to find it.

Perhaps your system is to put things on top of your desk so that you can take care of them later. Every time you look at your desk, you groan and go find something else to do. Later gets later and later. My downfall with that system comes when I am expecting company and clear off the desk by stuffing everything in a drawer. Out of sight, out of mind and a deadline goes by.

Low maintenance gardens mean less time spent in doing the gardening. Low maintenance organization of paperwork means more time for more pleasurable occupations.

Where to begin? Let's start with the important papers first. Where is your birth certificate? Where is your will? Where do you keep deeds and insurance policies? Could you grab them in case of fire? There is a person who makes his living by getting these types of papers in order for his clients. He charges a lot of money for the service. You can do it for yourself.

I suggest a safety deposit box for legal documents that are difficult to replace. For example, you should include birth and marriage certificates, passports, deeds, automobile pink slips, wills, and copies of your tax returns. Also, put in lists of all your credit card numbers, insurance policies, Social Security numbers, and an inventory of personal property with photographs of valuable items covered by your homeowners insurance. Photocopy everything that is in your deposit box so you have access to the information. Make a list of everything you carry in your wallet so that if you lose your wallet, you can replace your valuables. Credit card insurance is designed for people who are not organized. In order to apply for the insurance you have to give all the information to the credit card insurance company. In affect, you are forced to take the very action you are trying to avoid. Why not have this information even if you don't sign up for the insurance? Include the 800 numbers to call to report missing cards.

As you gather all these papers together, you may need to secure some information to make your collection complete. If you are missing your birth certificate, send for one now so that when you need one, say for a passport, you do not have a delay. It would be a real disappointment if you couldn't make the deadline and missed a trip.

Perhaps your will is outdated or you don't have one. This deserves your attention right away. Terrible consequences can happen to the dearest members of your family, such as not stating who the guardian of your children is to be. With all the combined families joined after divorces and the possibility of former spouses getting your assets, etc., it is even more complicated.

I know you don't like to think about the fact that your will is necessary at some point in time, but do it and get it over with so you are not guilty of neglect. Your will is a privilege you have to state how you want things to be distributed.

Always go to the right person for professional advice you need. Anything otherwise is hearsay. That includes members of your family who are quick with advice. Just smile and go see a professional.

Now that we have the biggies out of the way, we can get back to the immediate need to organize current information and bills. Sorting paper and putting it in order is great, but if it is not stored in a way to stay in order, or you have to go through the whole pile to get to one item, you are still not organized. File folders put into a box are the easiest to use and to grab during an emergency.

File folders come in colors and you can use different colors for different types of papers. For instance, use green folders for income and paycheck stubs, blue for bills, manila for information like equipment manuals, guarantees and general information, yellow for pleasurable information like vacation, travel, hobbies and future purchases. Paid bills could be put into a folder for the current year and into boxes, one for each year, for storage.

Keep paid bills, cancelled checks, pay stubs, and record keeping files for verifying tax returns, along with a copy of your return for at least three years; seven years if you want to be able to stand up to an audit from the IRS. Scary thought. It is up to the taxpayer to verify accuracy of information given for tax purposes. Guilty until proven innocent—not innocent until proven guilty. "If in doubt, keep it" is a good rule to follow. Having an accountant make out your return does not relieve you of the burden of proof as accountants can claim you did not give them correct or complete information.

(My parents' house burned to the ground and they had to reconstruct their income tax forms for three years prior to the fire. The IRS would not supply them with the information and it was a painful process for my father who was losing his eyesight. Because he was a CPA, he had made out his own tax forms. If he had had another accountant do it, there would have been copies available. Perhaps his experience influenced me to go into such detail.)

Are you getting tired just thinking about all this? Like the little boy who asked the librarian for information on alligators and she gave him six books: "This is a lot more than I want to know about alligators," he said. You may think these comments about organizing your personal finances is more than you wanted to know. If you do go for the whole system, you are going to feel so good! You might call it smug. After all, you will be one of very few who are well organized.

Here is my filing system that is simple and effective for me.

BEVERLEE KELLEY'S FILE SYSTEM
for Tons of Papers, Books, Binders, etc.

List Locations Where Information Is Stored

• You decide what locations and how many folders in each.

• There is no need for labels, but you may want to use them. (This system offers some privacy if you do not use labels.)

Desk Drawer. File numbers 1-15

Briefcase. File numbers 16-25

File Cabinet Drawer A. File numbers 26-52

File Cabinet Drawer B. File numbers 53-80

Book Shelf A. File numbers 81-86

Binders on Book Shelf B. (Treat divider tabs as files) numbers 87-102

Box in Trunk of Car. File numbers 103-125

Tote Bag. File numbers 126-133

Create An Index

Use a binder and list contents of files first in numeric order.

Column headings are:
File number, Location, Contents, Date (Optional)

Cross Index

Use dividers for the alphabet. Have an alphabetical listing of information for the purpose of finding items that could be the same yet named differently, i.e. Insurance under "I", Insurance company name under "first letter of name", Auto Insurance under "A". List in as many places as file contents could be named.

Column headings are:

Contents, File number, Location, Date (Optional)

Put Data in Folders or Binders

Number file folders starting with number 1 through however many you need. More numbers can be added later. Put information in numbered folders as you fill in the data in your index. For three-ring binders, give dividers each a file number as though they were folders if you will want to find specific contents.

The Advantages of This File System

The value of this file system is that contents of the files can be changed or added, then the folders do not need labels unless you desire, you can put things in appropriate locations, and you have a method of finding them, whether they are books, letters, papers, pictures or newspaper clippings.

NOTE: If you loan out materials, list who has what in your index.

Our next project is to balance the checkbook. Then we can start the COLORCODE CARD SYSTEM. Honest, it is coming up real soon.

SUMMARY

1. It takes time to be disorganized.

2. Important papers need to be put in proper places for protection and availability.

3. Update your will.

4. When you need legal advice, go to a professional.

5. Use file folders of different colors for different types of papers.

6. Keep records in case of an IRS audit.

7. Beverlee Kelley's File System.

Chapter Seven

HOW TO BALANCE YOUR CHECKBOOK

- It is unnecessary to have checks bounce.
- Six steps for balancing your checkbook.
- Develop credit before you need it.
- A good credit rating is important.

You and your bank should be friends. There are lots of ways to get your bank's attention and some of them are good for you. One thing you don't want is to receive a notice that you are overdrawn. One statistic I have heard is that one out of every fourteen checks written bounces and it is usually for an amount under twenty dollars. That would explain why banks no longer call a depositor when they are overdrawn. They would be calling people all day long.

You are fortunate if your bank calls you and you can get a deposit to them in time for them to honor the check that has insufficient funds behind it. What a waste of energy, rushing to the bank when you had other plans. You're upset as if it were the bank's fault, and you feel rotten 'cus you know it is your fault. Good grief Charlie Brown! I think your blood pressure is rising!

Heaven help you if you got a notice in the mail instead of a call. It arrives two or more days after the fact—you are charged the price of lunch out by the bank and a possible late charge or service charge by the company to whom you sent the check. Lucky you if there was only one check. Prevention is really easier than the cure. Knowing what you have in the bank before you give out a check is not difficult. It just takes a little time, less time than correcting an error.

"Why is it, that when you don't know how much money is in the bank, it is usually less than you need?"

The hard part is writing down the amount of each check as you write it so you know how much money you have spent. Some people don't like others to see their balance when they cash a check so they won't open their book to the registry while someone watches. Later, they forget to enter it. Another way to get into trouble is to carry blank checks in your wallet and not enter them in the "big book".

Calling the bank to see what your balance is can get you into trouble because their records may not include checks you have written that have not yet cleared the bank. You think you have $500.00 in the bank, but you don't know that your car payment check has not cleared. You write a check for $50.00 at the market and Zappo! the market calls two days later and asks you to please come in and make good the check. (Along with more charges.)

Promise yourself to fill in the stub before you write each check. I know it is a bore, but life offers enough drama without creating more. Also, you are holding up the line while you take a moment to do this, but it builds the confidence of the person waiting for your check that you are a responsible person.

One thing that confuses people in figuring their bank balance is the charges and automatic withdrawals that are deducted from their account. Treat these as if you wrote checks for those amounts. Enter those charges in your check registry. If you have a bank charge for $7.50 a month and do not keep tract of it for a year, you will think you have $90.00 that isn't there.

NOW FOR THE STEP-BY-STEP DETAIL ON HOW TO BALANCE YOUR CHECKBOOK.

1. Put your checks in numerical order.

2. Take your statement and check off each check on the statement, looking to see if each check is yours and all the checks are noted for the amount on the check.

3. Mark in your checkbook registry each check that has been returned to you. Add the withdrawals and bank charges. Is your total the same as the bank statement?

4. Mark off the deposits credited to you by matching the deposits slips you have kept. (Of course, you kept them.) Is your total the same as the bank statement?

If the balance in your check registry does not agree with your statement:

a. Is there an error in your addition or subtraction?

b. Were the bank charges included?

c. Was a deposit not included? (Happy Find!)

d. Voided checks (= $.00) or checks entered twice can confuse the problem. Are there check numbers that are missing?

If you cannot find your error, you can ask the bank to help you find a mistake.

Current Balance

1. On the back of your statement, list the checks that are missing and total their amount. These are outstanding checks. (Checks that have not cleared the bank.)

2. Subtract the outstanding checks from the ending balance on your statement.

3. Add any deposits made after the date of the statement to the ending balance on your statement. This is your current balance.

Computers do not make errors as often as people who give information to computers. If you find a problem, contact your bank as soon as possible. Do not be afraid to talk to the people at the bank. They are working for you. You are the customer. Get to know the tellers by name. They will begin to recognize you and can handle your transactions faster for not having to verify that you are who you are each time. Get to know the bank management and speak to them as often as you can. Building rapport now will make it easier for you when you want a loan.

Having an account in one bank for a number of years is a great advantage. You get extra points in your favor. When you cash a check at a store, the person okaying your check will notice the number of your check. If it is a low number of less than 100, you could be new in town or not have a good relationship with the last bank you used. That could mean trouble for the store.

DEVELOP A GOOD CREDIT RATING STARTING NOW

Paying cash for everything is a great discipline, but it is of no value when applying for a loan. Credit ratings are based on how you pay debts. Debts can be credit cards, loans, or 30-day charge accounts. "Debt" is not a bad word, if it is debt within reason (affordable). Adding debt when there are no funds to pay is "Bad Debt". Spending money you don't have or won't have can get you in trouble. Taking out loans and paying them off as agreed, or better than agreed, is smart.

Apply for an automatic overdraft loan service on your checking account. When you have written a check and do not have enough to cover it, your bank will automatically loan you the money. By paying the automatic loan off as soon as possible, you will build a good credit rating. When you want a car loan or a loan to pay your taxes, your good credit rating will help you. Credit bureaus and banks rate payments in three ways: As agreed—paid on time for the amount of the payment; Better than agreed—on time and for a larger amount then required; and Less than agreed—late and or less than the amount required. Paying even $10 more than the amount required is wise on your part. Paying double payments is better. Paying off the balance is best.

If you are thinking of making a commitment to pay so much a month, you would be wise to save that amount for three months to see if it is feasible before committing to something you will have trouble paying.

Applying for credit before you need it is easier than asking for a loan when you have to have it. If you take time to develop a credit rating that shows you are a good customer and are responsible, then should you have to have some help with a loan to pay taxes, or such, you can borrow more money than if you go in for the first time and ask for a loan.

To WANT a loan because of a decision you have made, like getting a new car or buying a home, is one thing. NEEDING a loan because you are short of cash is another. If your reputation shows you do not have checks bounce, you pay loans off on time or sooner then agreed, you stand a better chance of getting help when you NEED it. THE FACT THAT YOU HAVE DONE NOTHING WRONG IS MORE IMPORTANT THAN WHETHER OR NOT YOU HAVE SPENT MONEY WISELY.

Your bank will be asked for a credit reference if you apply for a loan elsewhere. It is very easy for the people you are dealing with to find out who your bank is—you probably gave them a check for a down payment and the information is on it. Usually they will ask you for your account number and the branch where you bank.

So balancing your checkbook is not just an exercise to see if you have money. It is an important part of developing good credit.

SUMMARY

1. One out of every fourteen checks bounce. It is not necessary in most cases. Prevention is easier than the cure.

2. Write on your stub the amount of every check and to whom it is paid before you write your check.

3. Calling the bank to see if you have money in your account is risky. There may be checks that have not cleared.

4. Treat bank charges and automatic payments as though you had written a check for that amount.

5. There are five steps to balancing your checkbook and three more to get your current balance.

6. Get to know the people at your bank and let them know you.

7. Stay with one bank for added points on your credit rating.

8. Apply for credit before you need it.

9. Balancing your checkbook is important to having a good credit rating.

Chapter Eight

THE COLORCODE CARD SYSTEM

- The COLORCODE CARD SYSTEM encourages you to keep records.
- How to implement the system.
- Information gathered in one place.
- The COLORCODE CARD SYSTEM is flexible.

This is the plan I have been referring to throughout the book. It is easier than using columns of numbers in a book. It is more flexible; if you make a mistake, you can throw that card away and start a new one. Important information is in one place. New cards can be added for new expenses. Completed cards of bills paid off can be set aside. The cards can be rearranged in a different order as you make decisions to pay them sooner or pay more than required to reduce you debt. And your records are more complete.

What is encouraging about using this card system is that you can see the progress you are making every time you pay a bill. We need all the encouragement we can get in this world, right?

I use 5 X 8 cards because I write large and the advantage to you is that more information can be put on each card than on the usual column–type record keeping systems. Plus it is all in one place.

The different colors for each type of bill or expense makes it more interesting as you will see when I explain what color I use for ordinary expenses, payments that bring added value, and bills that are debts.

Now for the particulars. You will need a supply of cards in colors of green, white, blue, yellow, and bright pink (which henceforth I will call red, OK?). These are standard colors available at stationery stores. Get index cards with tabs or buy plastic tabs and apply them. You will need at least fifteen; twelve for the months of the year, one for the first of the month, one for the 15th of the month, and one for cards that are inactive. If you are paid once a week, you may want to have four tabs instead of two for each month. Four times a year you will have an extra week which is a bonus. Also you will want to have a card file box to keep them in. (Purchase another 12 white cards for the cash flow project coming next.)

Note: In the back of this book you will find masters for copying on to your colored 5 x 8 cards. (You can use them as they are if you can not wait to get to the stationary store.) You may need more cards than provided—so photocopy them and you will be able to use the masters again next year.

Cards are used horizontally. Each card will be used each week, month or quarter for a year or more.

The first card you make out is for your savings account. Use a green card.

In the upper left hand corner, write the name of where you deposit your savings. This can be a Savings and Loan, bank, credit union, or the automatic withdrawal from your paycheck. (A "paycheck" can be income from a pension, Social Security or other source.) Write the address and telephone number for requesting information, account number; and the amount you want to save during one year.

```
SAVINGS ACCOUNT     Account Information: 619  555-1212          14th of the Month
Bank Name           Account # 55A6783 21                                $50.00
Address             Manager:  Ron Green            12 Months Goal  $600.00
City, State Zip
        Date        Check #          Amount          Balance

      Jan. 14       2071             $50             $50.00
      Feb. 14       2106             $50             $100.00
      Mar.14        2189             $50             $150.00




            GREEN CARD
            FOR ASSETS SUCH AS SAVING,
            MORTGAGE, IRAS, ETC.
```

In the upper right–hand corner put the day of the month, such as the number 17, or third Friday, when you are going to make your deposit. Under that put the amount you plan to deposit.

The heading across the card for the entries you make should be: date, check #, amount of deposit, and new balance. You can see all in one place what you need on this one card. There will be no need to hunt through all the papers to figure out when you last deposited, or how much you have, etc. To add the interest you receive, simply put the date, make a notation under the check number column "interest earned", the amount, and your new balance.

The first card is the hardest. Just getting the information together may cause stress, but hang in there! You may not have a savings account yet, but I hope you will, and soon. The first person you pay should be yourself. Every month when you go through your bills, you can see how much you are gaining in your savings. Add more than you planned, when you can. Perhaps on the four fifth weeks of the year.

The next green card is for the mortgage payment, if you are so lucky to own your own home. Again, put the information at the upper left side: name of mortgage company, address, phone, loan number; the amount of the loan when you first got it, the current debt still to pay, and the percentage of interest you are paying. To give yourself a lift, put down the current market value of your home.

In the upper right–hand side of the card put the day of the month you make your payment. (Allow for mail time and put a date ahead of the due date.) The amount goes under the day.

The column entries across the card are: date, check number, amount of principle, amount of interest, balance due, and the right–hand column shows the difference between your market value and what you owe. That last figure is part of your net worth!

Make out another green card for each permanent life insurance policy you have if you pay monthly. You will make out a red card if you pay less often than monthly. Again, the identifying information goes in the upper left-hand corner, day or date to pay, and the amount goes in the upper right.

The entries for columns are: date, check #, amount, and cash value of the policy. You may have to call and find out what this figure is from time to time, at least once a year. First look on your premium billing.

As you can see, green cards are for assets. All the investments and savings go on green cards. I hope you need a lot of green cards for your COLORCODE CARD SYSTEM!

Green cards come first. They represent your future and your present monetary worth. Green is your prosperous color. Love that green stuff!

ELECTRIC CO.	Billing Information: 619 555-1212		1st of the Month
Address	Emergency Phone #		12 Months Last year $780.00
City, State Zip			
Date	**Check #**	**Amount**	**Year to Date**
Jan. 1	2075	$65.00	$65.00

WHITE CARDS
FOR UTILITIES, TELEPHONE, PAID UP
CREDIT CARDS, ETC.

White cards are for the monthly bills that do not carry forward a balance due. The value of paying these bills is a good credit rating, but they do not have asset values in themselves. Your rent would be recorded on a white card, as well as your utilities. These bills can vary in amount due, such as your heating bill. Keeping track of what you spend is a big part of the plan and you need to know how much you spend during the year. Department store charge accounts and credit cards will be recorded on white cards IF YOU PAY THE TOTAL BALANCE EACH MONTH. This is the goal: not to be in debt and not to pay finance charges. The identifying information should be on each card so you can call if you have an inquiry. This is especially important if you have to report a lost charge card or credit card.

AUTO LOAN	Account Information: 619 555-1212			14th of the Month
Bank Name	Account #43 A 56789			$350.00
Address	Term 4 years			12 Months $4200.
City, State Zip	$4,000.00			

Date	Check #	Amount	Principal	Interest	Balance
Jan. 14	2073	$350	$267.00	$33.00	$3967.00

BLUE CARDS
FOR DEBTS SUCH AS CREDIT CARD
BALANCES, LOANS, ETC.

Blue cards are next. Blue is appropriate as you can be blue thinking about them. Hopefully, you will have fewer and fewer blue cards as you use this system over the months ahead. Blue cards are for debts, such as loans or credit cards, that have an unpaid balance for more than thirty days and accounts for purchases that are on time payments. Remember one or two loans for developing a good credit rating are OK, but too many monthly payments are a negative.

Blue card column entries are: date, check number, amount paid, and balance still owed. Enter current charges as you make them and note the amount of available credit you have. The last number will go up as you pay off your debt.

On the blue cards for credit purchases, note the billing date at the top of the card so you can delay charging new purchases until after that day and it will give you more time to pay. (But not less interest to pay, your daily balance is what you pay interest on.) Again, send more than the amount required for two reasons: one, to lower your debt, and two, to get a good credit rating. Remember to allow for mail delivery and don't miss paying on time. One advantage of our system is to know when you need to send your check.

ALLOWANCE			$75.00 a week
Cash			12 months $3900.00
Date	Check #	Amount	Total to Date
Jan. 3	2072	$75	$75.00
Jan. 10	2107	$75	$150.00
Jan. 17	2190	$75	$225.00

YELLOW CARDS
FOR PLEASURABLE THINGS SUCH AS VACATIONS, CLOTHES, ALLOWANCE, HOBBIES, ETC.

Yellow cards are more fun! Yellow is for the pleasurable things we do, like spending the money in your wallet. You can call it your allowance if you like. You don't have to keep track of it if that is too much even though it is helpful information when you want to restrict how much you spend. All you need to know is when the money will be replenished. Then you can decide if you can go ahead and buy something you like, or go out to lunch, or plan a weekend trip.

Everybody needs cash in hand to pay for little things. When you are planning your system, be sure not to overlook the need for cash. Some people are inclined to plan so tight a budget that they have to act tight themselves. There is enough stress about the concerns of money without wondering if you have enough for a parking meter.

We have one more color card to face and then we can get to the part that tells us what we can do about these bills. (That will be the CASH FLOW CHART.) So hang in there and let's get to the biggies—the red cards.

SAVINGS ACCOUNT Bank Name Address City, State Zip	Account Information: 619 555-1212 Account # 55A6783 21 Manager: Ron Green	14th of the Month $50.00 12 Months Goal $600.00

Date	Check #	Amount	Balance
Jan. 14	2071	$50	$50.00
Feb. 14	2106	$50	$100.00
Mar.14	2189	$50	$150.00

RED CARDS

FOR HOLIDAYS, BIRTHDAYS, AUTO
INSURANCE AND OTHER PERIODIC
EXPENSES

The red cards are for expenditures that come less frequently than once a month. The expenses that are difficult to handle if you are not prepared. Automobile insurance, taxes, large purchases, birthday gifts, anniversary presents, celebrations, vacations and Christmas. This is the part of the COLORCODE CARD SYSTEM that really pays off.

Each one of those "events" is put on a separate red card. Put the name of the expense you anticipate in the upper left-hand corner of the card. Underneath, put the amount. Put the date that you anticipate the expense will be due in the upper-left hand corner. Count the number of pay periods before that expense is due and divide the total into that many parts. THIS IS THE AMOUNT YOU NEED TO PUT INTO A RESERVE ACCOUNT.

A separate savings account will keep track of this for you. You will be drawing out funds from this account, so make sure there is no penalty for withdrawing money. Some financial institutions limit withdrawals you can make and charge you if you make more than that. You need only one savings account for the total of all the red cards. If you want more than one savings account, that is OK, too. It might be the way you get around the withdrawal limitation.

So now you have a card for every expense. You decide what color card you want to put your grocery money on, yellow for cash out-of-pocket, or white, and keep that money separate. You decide what you want to do about clothes; will you always buy them at a department store and charge them? That may cost you more than paying cash and being able to shop anywhere. You decide how you want to pay for household needs, auto repairs, and such. It is really your card system now, not mine.

Everyone has different situations to handle. It is not my place to tell you if you are spending too much on housing. At one time, it was thought the percentage of income that could be spent on housing was thirty percent. A single person in an entry-level-job would have a hard time keeping to that mark. You may have expenses that others do not, such as medication for a chronic illness, or you may have young people in college. Few young people can afford to pay their own way and most who rely on parents' money have no intention of paying back what it costs.

The COLORCODE CARD SYSTEM is an information system that tells you what is happening to your money and what you can afford.

The following guide will show what I use. Make your COLORCODE CARD SYSTEM GUIDE for what you need.

Savings	Green
IRA	Green
Car Loan	Green (Car is an asset)
Refrigerator Payment	Blue (yes, it will be an asset when I pay it off, but I would have a hard time getting what I paid for it.)
Rent	White
Electric Co.	White
Gas Co.	White
Newspaper	White
Food	White
Cleaning	White
Credit Card	White (30 days) or Blue (Payments)
Department Store	White (30 days) or Blue (Payments)
Gasoline Credit Card	White (30 days) or Blue (Payments)
Allowance	Yellow
Clothes	Yellow
Christmas	Red
Birthdays	Red
Auto Insurance	Red
Renter's Insurance	Red
Estimated Taxes	Red

SUMMARY

1. The COLORCODE CARD SYSTEM is encouraging to you because it shows how much you are gaining.

2. A 5 X 8 card file and 5 X 8 colored cards in green, red, white, blue, and yellow are needed as well as index cards with tabs.

3. Each card will have all the information on it for each bill, should you have to call to report missing credit cards or need to know an interest figure for your records.

4. The red cards show how much is needed in a reserve account for the surprise of costly events.

5. The COLORCODE CARD SYSTEM is flexible and each person who puts it into operation makes it fit his or her unique circumstances.

CASH FLOW CARDS
January

Date: 1st			Date: 15th		
Balance in Checking Acct.	$		Balance Carried Forward	$	
+ Income	$		+ Income	$	
Subtotal Available		+ $	Subtotal Available		+ $
Expenses	$		Expenses	$	
+ Reserve Acct. Savings	$		+ Reserve Acct. Savings	$	
Subtotal of Money out		- $	Subtotal of Money out		- $
Balance = Subtotal Available Minus Subtotal of Money Out		= $	Balance = Subtotal Available Minus Subtotal of Money Out		= $

(Make out cards for each month. Have four columns if income is weekly)

CASH FLOW CARDS
February

Date: 1st			Date: 15th		
Balance Carried Forward	$		Balance Carried Forward	$	
+ Income	$		+ Income	$	
Subtotal Available		+ $	Subtotal Available		+ $
Expenses	$		Expenses	$	
+ Reserve Acct. Savings	$		+ Reserve Acct. Savings	$	
Subtotal of Money out		- $	Subtotal of Money out		- $
Balance = Subtotal Available Minus Subtotal of Money Out		= $	Balance = Subtotal Available Minus Subtotal of Money Out		= $

Chapter Nine

THE CASH FLOW CHART

- See a problem before it is a crisis.
- Cash flow charts do your worrying for you.
- How one woman got out of financial trouble.

The mystery is about to be solved! The cash flow chart is going to pull it all together and give us the answer to how much we are spending, how much we need, and what can be expected. We are going to put all our bills into time slots of when we pay them and balance that with our income.

We might find a problem which will be discussed in the very next chapter, or we might find we have money to go into a major purchase or investment. We will be able to see which months are overloaded with expenses and if some months show a surplus. Having a reserve account for the red cards should even that problem out, but let's see what happens.

Make a white card for each month of the year, for a total of twelve cards.

Take the card for the current month. On the left hand side, write in: Date, Balance, Income, Cash on Hand, Sub-total Available, Expenses, Reserve Acct. Savings, Sub-total of Money Out, and Balance.

If you receive income twice a month, then draw a line down the middle of the remaining blank space of the card. If you are receiving income weekly, then draw lines to divide the space into four or five sections, one for each week in that month. Check your calendar to see how many weeks are in each month so that you wil have a column for each income period. Enter figures.

To get the figures you need, start with the balance in your checkbook (which you already have figured using the "How to Balance your Checkbook" chapter). Put that figure next to Balance (in Checking Acct.) at the top of the first column.

The Income figure is any source of funds such as your paycheck. If you borrow money—Heaven forbid—include that in the Income figure. Whenever you take money out of your reserve account for paying a red card expense, that also goes into the Income figure. Add the Checking Acct. amount and Income amount for Sub-total Available.

Sort your 5 x 8 expense cards into piles by due date. Any due dates that fall before the next income period go in one pile. Total your expenses. Include your regular savings account, not the reserve account, as one of your expenses. Include a red card expense if it is due during this pay period. Enter the amount to go into your Reserve Account Savings. Total these items for Money Out.

Subtract Money Out from the Subtotal Available for the Balance. Carry forward the last figure for Balance to the top of the next pay period.

You may have a larger amount for income in one pay period than another. Most paychecks have fewer deductions during one of the pay periods. This is not true for everyone, but happens often.

Go through the steps again. The reserve account may have just one entry a month from only one pay period, or perhaps you will put part of the amount needed into the reserve account each pay period. You decide.

When you have completed this card, start the next month with the total from the last of the preceding month and complete all twelve cards.

Perhaps I should have mentioned it before, but now that you see the system, it is easier for you to see the importance of the reserve account. WHEN YOU PAY THE EXPENSE OF A RED CARD, MAKE A NEW CARD IMMEDIATELY. If you have twelve months before it is due again, then divide the total expense by twelve, to know how much to add to your reserve account.

When you first start this system, you have some catching up to do for not having saved to cover expenses which are due soon. After working with the system a year, you will not have that burden and it is much easier.

Evaluate what you have done. Do you have any times when you do not have enough money to pay the expenses? How much more do you need? Did you have money left over? If your last card of twelve months shows a large surplus, you can see that you can put more into savings or into an investment. If you are still paying accounts that are over 30 days, then use your surplus to pay those bills off. The sooner you do, the sooner the finance charges will stop.

The cash flow chart can give you advance warning of trouble ahead. THE SOONER YOU KNOW, THE SOONER YOU CAN TAKE ACTION TO AVOID CRISIS.

I know that having a cash flow chart works. I once had a friend who was really in bad financial straits. She was raising three children alone. Her ex-husband did not often send the support checks. She had a foreign car that quit running and needed $500.00 for repairs. She had just put $300.00 into it for other repairs. She had a job that required at least fifty miles of driving a day, so she bought another car and quit making payments on the first one. Soon, the credit union was after her for back payments and she was getting scared.

Her children were always begging for money or new clothes and she was tired of saying she could not afford it. Plus she felt guilty about not giving them more. She was buying food meal by meal and going to fast-food places because it was easier. She got a second job to add to her income, but whenever she had cash in her pocket, she would buy something she thought she needed because she felt depressed.

I developed a plan for her such as you have just done for yourself. She was able to hold her head up high and talk to the credit union who had the loan on the first car. They gave her a longer term loan to pay it off, took the old car and junked it.

She gave herself just enough cash for spending money, kept the food money separate so she spent more wisely, set aside a certain amount to spend on the children and held to just that. Within eight months, she was able to ease up a little. Within a year and a half, she was going to ski resorts and enjoying mini-vacations. By then, she did not have to hold down two jobs and she was much more relaxed than she had been since being on her own.

One of the biggest changes she made was not spending the money she had after paying the bills that were due immediately. Instead, she kept money for the bills that were coming. It was absolutely necessary in order to not get farther behind. The cash flow chart did her worrying for her. Before, she had everything in her head about what might happen.

It was a hard lesson to live through, but she has proven to herself that she can control her spending and get more for her money.

You may have a special ace in the hole, not mentioned before, which is your income tax refund. That might bail you out of difficulty. It would be smart to have your income tax figured early in January so you can send it in early if you have a refund, or send it by the fifteenth of April if you have to pay. Use your income tax refund to build your reserve account, pay off credit-over-thirty-days accounts, or start another savings account for a special purchase.

It takes a lot of time and concentration to get ready for your new plan, but you are to be commended for giving all that energy to start taking control. You will have fewer worries as your reward for all this effort.

Most businesses use a system similar to this cash flow chart, but very few people do it for themselves. You are way ahead of the crowd for having taken the time to figure out all these details. The cards you have completed are really estimates. You may have forgotten an expense. You may not have anticipated how much you really spend. In order to really control your personal finances, you will want to make out a cash flow card each month with what actually was paid out, saved in the reserve, and what you really got on your paycheck. I hope you got a raise and all your income figures are underestimated!

The following chapters will help you avoid expenses that are unnecessary and help you to save money. Anyone with hard cash is going to enjoy some real opportunities. Anyone without reserves is going to have a hard time of it. The time to take control is NOW!

SUMMARY

1. A cash flow chart will balance expenses against income.

2. You can see a problem before it is a crisis.

3. Making up a card for each month shows if you have enough income or cash left over at the end of the year.

4. Cash flow charts do your worrying for you.

5. Businesses use cash flow charts similar to this but very few people know to do it for themselves.

6. Your ace in the hole may be your income tax refund. When you have a cash flow chart, you know whether or not you can freely spend it or if you need to save your refund for future expenses.

Chapter Ten

OH, DEAR—YOU ARE OVERDRAWN!

- What to do if you are in over your head.
- How to handle bill collectors.
- Don't let "the times" influence your thinking.

Perhaps, after you really look at your income and your expenses, you find you are in a position of being unable to keep up with your obligations. What do you do if you are in over your head?

This book is not the place for legal advice. However, there are books written by attorneys that will explain what you can do. Go to the library and you can find lists of organizations that counsel people with money problems. Please don't take bankruptcy as the way out until you have really had objective advice. The cost of living goes up for all of us when people do not pay their bills.

What if the bill collectors are knocking at your door? Does that make you a rotten person? Not necessarily. If you were a rotten person, you would have skipped town, changed your name several times, and committed criminal acts. Even then you might not be rotten, just desperate.

Sure, you regret your present circumstances. Sure, you could have done differently. Sure, you have pride. So what's new? As long as you are earning money or have an income, you can improve your situation.

The most uncomfortable part about being in debt is having to deal with people who are trying to get you to pay them money when you don't have it. We don't like what they are thinking about us. Many people assume that when someone does not pay a bill, they are dishonest. Not having enough money does not mean you are dishonest. It only means you do not have enough money. A person who commits to pay a sum and then does not when they do have funds might be dishonest; but the person who does not write a bad check is more honest than the one who pretends there are funds and does.

The obnoxious creditor who acts rude, aggressive, and very selfish has lost faith that softer, kinder ways will bring the desired results. The creditor has the problem. How you respond either gives more frustration or relieves their anger. Probably the best you can do, if you are not able to pay your creditors in full, is to reduce their anger. If your responses are motivated by as much frustration as theirs, then you will aggravate them and see them in court.

If indeed you agree with them that you do owe the money, then the next thing to do is to show your intent to pay. Develop a plan that will allow you to pay part of the amount on a regular basis.

You have just had to face a disagreeable experience. What can you do to keep your sanity? Remember the basic theory that a person and their actions are separate. The child who acts mean is not a mean child, but a child who feels like being mean. You are not a bad person; in fact, you are probably too nice and that is what got you into trouble. You wanted to do more than you could.

Fear immobilizes positive action. Reduce your fear. The world will still keep on turning, you will eat another meal, you will have a place to stay, and life goes on. You will have learned a valuable lesson if you solve this problem.

Most people who go into bankruptcy could have paid all their debts in four or five years. Most of those people owed less than the price of a new car.

Better you should spend some time enjoying the sunset than to worry. If you never do anything until you are worried about it, then go ahead and worry. No one said you had to be perfect. Just avoid doing wrong. Think of yourself as successful and this time circumstances are temporary.

To reverse the trend of spending more than your income, there are two things you can do. The first is to cut expenses. There are three chapters following this one that will give you ideas. The other way is to increase income. Let's talk about generating additional income.

Looking at your present employment, can you improve your income? Can you seek a promotion or promote more income by becoming more efficient at what you are now doing? Do you need to take courses to improve your skills? Do you need to make up a new resumé and seek a better paying job in your field? If you are self-employed, do you think it might be wise to work for somebody else for awhile? If you are employed, could you make more money on your own as a consultant? That last question is tricky because if you are in financial difficulty and you start a new business on your own, you are starting from a very weak position.

Perhaps a second job is an answer for you. Getting a second job is a real commitment to paying your bills. Can you be sure to get enough rest? Can your family get along if you are gone more hours each day? Will they cooperate? If you can keep the vision of getting your bills paid and not resent "having to work so hard," a second job is the fastest way to get ahead.

Generating more cash can be a very creative adventure. Check your skills, both household skills and business skills. Offering services to others for a fee can be the least expensive in start-up costs. That is, you don't need to purchase expensive equipment. Anything from washing windows to keeping books for someone else can bring you cash. If you are too embarrassed to offer your services in your own neighborhood, go to another area close by to canvas for opportunity. There is nothing wrong with letting people know you are interested in accummulating extra cash. In fact, it is admired.

Garage sales are fun and your unnecessary clutter goes away. Clutter is so depressing. It is in the way and affects your thinking more than you know. If there is never a clear space on the kitchen counter, it is hard to want to cook something that takes preparation. If there is no desk or tabletop clear, it is hard to do paperwork. Some people move to a different apartment or house because they think they do not have enough space, when all they need to do is throw out the unnecessary junk. One man's junk is another man's prize. Garage sales are great!

Garage sales can have another asset which can be used to your benefit. A woman in real estate held a garage sale whenever she could gather enough stuff to sell. She made contacts for listing houses and she made a million dollar sale to one of the friendly people who came to her garage. Do you have a service you want to advertise? Have a garage sale and tell everyone who comes what you do. Swap meets are even better for seeing lots of people and getting prospects.

During the Depression, some people made fortunes. During prosperous years, lots of people went broke. Don't let "the times" influence your thinking. You can be a winner.

SUMMARY

1. What to do if you are in over your head.

2. How to handle the bill collectors.

3. Keep your sanity while facing a difficult situation.

4. Reduce your fear as fear immobilizes positive action.

5. Most people who elect bankruptcy could have paid their debts in four to five years.

6. Cutting expenses and generating more income are two ways to remedy going into debt.

7. Don't let "the times" influence your thinking.

Chapter Eleven

CREDIT CARDS

- The advantages of credit cards.
- Watch your billing date.
- Protect your cards.

I am not against credit cards. Credit cards give you flexibility in making purchases when you do not have enough cash with you. They are instant money and you don't have to pay the bill until later. Each purchase you make is an automatic loan.

What I am against is paying finance charges unnecessarily. The practical use of credit cards has the advantage of delaying payment up to as much as forty-five days, and the record of what you spent is recorded on your bill. This is handy, particularly if you use one card for personal expenses and another one for business expenses. However, going past the forty-five days costs money, which is cash spent for nothing.

Another advantage is you don't have to carry cash in large amounts. You can take advantage of sales. When you see something you need that is on sale, your credit card gives you the funds needed with no delay. The money you save, 25 to 50 percent, is even worth a finance charge if you must.

Not having to carry large amounts of cash is a real advantage when you travel, especially to a foreign country. The conversion of American dollars to the foreign currency is automatically done for you by the credit card people, but it does cost you for the service. Find out how much it costs by calling your credit card company.

Credit cards also help you establish a credit rating. My father was a CPA. He kept records of every penny spent. (No wonder I don't like budgets!) When he came close to retirement, he applied for an American Express card. He was really surprised when they turned him down. No one could have been a better credit risk! It did not seem fair to him at all. The reason he was turned down was he had no credit history.

He resented the fact that charge customers were considered preferred customers of department stores. He thought there should be a discount for paying cash, since businesses gained by not having to wait for their money and did not have to pay the percentage fee charged to merchants who use the credit card service. He was right. I have heard of businesses that do give a discount for cash, but since the public does not ask for it, they don't offer to take less than the marked price.

Credit cards are a disadvantage to the immature, self-indulgent persons who do not control their spending and charge more than is reasonable for their incomes, and the spenders who like to show off and impress others with their buying power. Those people are the ones who should not have a card.

How you use your credit cards tells a lot about how you control your spending. If you have gone overboard and used too much of your available credit, don't cut the cards and throw them away. Simply put them in a safe place until you get your balance down to where you can pay it off within the thirty days.

Paying off the balance on your credit card takes two years if you only pay the minimum amount due. Pay more than the minimum as often as you can. The interest or finance charge makes everything you bought thirty-five percent more expensive if you take so long to pay for it. That is like paying next years prices for something you bought last year.

Do not assume that because you have paid more than asked for several months in a row, you can skip a month. Any time you do not pay a percentage of the balance, a red flag goes up on your account. If you delay further, you might get a call and someone will ask you, "We need to verify the information on your application. Do you still work for the same company? Oh? Where do you work now? How long have you been employed there? In that case, please do not use your card until the balance is reduced." Who wants conversations like that?

Three times in my life I have been between "incomes". My credit cards helped me to get through the lean times. Ironically, it was at one of these times that I received a new credit card in the mail which I had not applied for with a $1,000 credit limit. And I received a letter from a current card that said they had increased my limit to $700 from $500. If I had applied for a card at that time, I could not have qualified for one. The moral of the story is: DON'T LET RED FLAGS SHOW UP ON YOUR ACCOUNT!

When you are making out a financial statement listing your assets, your unused credit amounts can be listed as part of your assets. Reserves such as your unused credit are very valuable. That is one reason not to close an account if at all possible. You don't have to use a credit card just because you have one. The membership fee can be worth the advantage of having emergency funds.

Protect yourself. Your credit card statement can have errors. When you first receive it, see if all the charges are ones you have made, and the amounts agree with the slips you have. No sense in accepting debt that you did not incur

While you have your statement in hand, mark the billing date on the back of your card. New purchases made after that date will go on the next statement. It is wise to delay a purchase to take advantage of the longer amount of time for paying it off.

If you have no accumulated balance from one statement to the next, you can delay your payment until the last minute and gain time to pay. If you have not paid off your balance, then pay as soon as possible because the finance charge is based upon the daily average of your balance. It comes to a lesser amount if you pay at the beginning of the cycle.

It also is to your advantage to pay one card off completely as soon as possible. When that one is paid fully, pay off another one with larger than minimum payments. You will be encouraged as you see your progress. The balance on the second card will get lower more quickly when you no longer have to make several different payments.

Use cash for all purchases until you have a card that does not have a balance carried forward. If you use a card that has been paid off, pay the full amount on the next bill or you will be right back in trouble again.

Credit cards are great! Prize them and protect them. On your COLORCODE CARD SYSTEM, have all the information you need if you have to report them stolen. List all of your account numbers in your safety deposit box.

The next three chapters are all about saving money. It takes money to save money. Saving money can be a very creative challenge.

SUMMARY

1. Credit cards have several advantages IF you pay off the total balance each month and avoid finance charges.

2. Credit cards help you establish a credit rating.

3. Paying off large balances can take two years if you pay only the minimum.

4. Paying more than the minimum does not give you the privilege of missing a payment. A red flag goes up if you miss.

5. Keep track of billing dates and postpone new purchases until after the billing date to gain time.

6. Pay off one card as soon as you can and then concentrate on the next one.

7. Protect your cards by having account numbers and telephone numbers on your COLORCODE CARD SYSTEM.

Chapter Twelve

SAVING MONEY BY SPENDING IT

- Buying items on sale saves money.
- Buying before need saves money.
- Convenience of having what you need saves money.

Surprised? You have probably done this many times and just didn't look at it this way. Any time you buy something on sale that you would have bought anyway, you have saved money. If you buy something on sale but you do not usually buy the item, then once again, the merchant got you to spend money.

Any time you buy in quantity at a discount or before prices go up, you have saved money by spending it. When you buy a year's supply of paper towels and then the price goes up, you have saved. For one thing, you have bought something you will be using anyway. The money you spent would not go towards something less useful, and you have gained the difference of prices now and prices later. The best part is you do not pay taxes on this kind of gain. The gain can be more than the amount of interest you would have earned, plus interest is taxable.

Four months ago, an item I bought was 80¢ and I stocked up. Now it is 99¢. By buying in advance of need, the savings was 11% in four months. In order to have a tax-free gain of four months time, I would have to invest my money at somewhere near 40%. It would be hard to find an investment that paid that well on less than $100.

The convenience of having what you need on hand is valuable also. There is the extra trip to the store, which takes money and time, and you feel so much more prosperous if you have reserves. This idea will not work if you buy something you do not like or will not use. Also, you might increase your expenses if you use more of the item because it is handy.

It is wise to have your eye out for clothes you will need in the future. If you are invited to a wedding and do not have something to wear, more likely than not, you will pay full price and spend more than you want. Now, add in the cost of the wedding present, and you wish the couple would just live together and not put you to all this expense. That is not the attitude to have when you go to a wedding!

Obviously, buying gifts ahead of need can save you money also. The clever item is often not as expensive as the traditional gift. Buying gifts while traveling makes your trip all the more fun and pleases the receiver as well. Again, if you wait until the deadline to shop, you will spend more money.

More and more people are using coupons to reduce their grocery bill. It is fashionable to use coupons and thought of as the smart thing to do. Some markets give double credit which makes it worthwhile for your effort. Ask yourself before you use a coupon—would another brand have cost you less? Would you normally buy the item? If you are spending more in order to use the coupon, then it is not saving you money.

One other way to cut your "food" bill is to simplify your household cleaners to some of the basic ingredients used for cleaning, such as vinegar or ammonia for cleaning glass and dry soda for cleaning chrome appliances such as toasters. One of the most effective cleansers for tile grouting and stoves is your dishwasher detergent.

The cost of packaging and scent add to the cost of the basic item. And items sold as useful for only one purpose are usually a waste of money. Instead of buying a coffee pot cleaner, use the dishwasher detergent and run through a cycle just as if you were making coffee. Rinse well and see it gleam.

A lot of articles are now being written that advise against permanent life insurance policies. They say, "Buy term and invest the difference." What they don't say is all the money you put into a term policy goes down the drain if you stop paying the premiums or premiums become so expensive as you get older, it is not a bargain.

Most people do not invest what they don't spend, so they have nothing. A person who buys a permanent insurance policy never has to pay more for the premium, and the policy stays in effect for as long as you live. If you stop paying premiums, you still have a lesser amount of paid-up insurance so your money is not wasted.

And the most important feature is that you can borrow all the cash values at a low percent of interest. That is a real advantage. Future insurance contracts will probably not have this low interest feature. The best thing is you don't have to pay the loan back. It is subtracted from the face of the policy.

By buying permanent insurance and borrowing cash values, you can pay as little in premiums as if you had bought term insurance. If you have a policy from a participating insurance company, as opposed to a stock holder insurance company, you will be receiving dividends. The advantage of having dividends is after approximately fourteen years your accumulated dividends will pay all the future premiums.

All those financial advisors who say buy term are assuming that you will have such a large estate when you die that you won't need insurance. That will happen for only 10% of the population.

Buying quality clothes is an investment that pays off. Those who buy inexpensive clothing do not feel prosperous, and spend as much money as if they had spent wisely by buying more clothes. Fashion experts know how to make basic wardrobes into stylish outfits by the attractive use of up-to-date accessories. Accessories such as shoes and hose wear out as well as go out of style. By replacing the accessories, such as ties and shirts for men, shoes and jewelry for women, up-to-date looks are accomplished. Spending for quality suits and dresses is a way to save money.

Furniture is another investment where quality pays off. Lamps, pillows, and even wallpaper and paint can be changed for a refreshing and up-to-date look. The basic styles of furniture do not change as often. They are still using furniture styles that were designed three hundred years ago.

"It takes money to make money" fits right in with saving money by spending. How clever you are if you have learned this lesson well.

SUMMARY

1. Buying things on sale is saving money if you need and use what you buy.

2. Buying in quantity ahead of need saves spending higher prices later.

3. Savings from buying at a discount are not taxable.

4. Shopping near the deadline of need often costs more money than buying ahead of need.

5. Convenience of having what you need on hand is a savings of money and time. You also feel more prosperous.

6. Spending more now for quality may save you much more in the long term.

7. Permanent insurance costs less than term except in the first few years.

8. Buying quality furniture, clothes and other items saves you money.

Chapter Thirteen

SAVING MONEY BY NOT SPENDING IT

- Save millions—don't buy.
- Some luxuries are necessary.
- The importance of feeling prosperous while limiting expenses.

I have saved millions of dollars and so have you by not spending money for everything the advertisers and my friends have suggested. There are some people who have to own everything they like. It may not be used often. It may not be easy to care for and deteriorate before it has served its purpose. It may be in the way and it may limit how you spend your time

For instance, you own a vacation home. Wonderful! You really enjoy going to the lake every time you have the chance. Great! You don't mind that it is vacant most of the time, exposed to vandalism and natural disasters, plus requires the normal cost of upkeep. Then do it. Yet, when you pay taxes and are not free to go anywhere else because you should go to the lake and fix the plumbing, then to me it is a burden and not an asset.

I see lots of boats every day. I live on a bay and those yachts are expensive critters. The definition of a boat is a hole in the water you pour money into. I love to see them and admire everything about them.

Except, I have the distinct advantage of not having to scrub the decks and polish the brass. Being around things of wealth is all I require. I bless those who clean, polish, and take friends out fishing when the cost of fuel may be $1500.00 for the weekend. My feeling is that the more people who can afford to do those things, the better off all of us are, and the closer we are to enjoying it with them.

There is one more thing I have found to be true. Spectators, guests, admirers, and appreciators are needed by these people in order for them to enjoy their investment. The point is, you do not have to own to enjoy.

There are things I enjoy owning that are not anything more than self-indulgence: my two-hundred-year-old Japanese table, the silver tea service my friends gave me, and a few other things that make my home...my home. I don't mind the extra care that they need so I can see why and how someone can want to own expensive "toys". But to have to own everything you like is out of proportion and not always wise.

I have read almost every book written on positive thinking. I love to read them. Such enthusiastic people wrote those books. They tell about miracles of unexpected money showing up at just the right time to the widow who had nothing. And I believe what they say is true. There have been lots of miracles in my life. However, my practical side says, "Don't spend money you don't have". Therefore, I don't spend money that is not within my power to spend freely. Spending and then feeling frightened about how the debt is to be paid is not freedom.

While you are trying to save money by not spending it, what will make you feel prosperous? What will encourage you to feel good and not limited? Make a list of pleasures that you have and ones you can be aware of which generate a prosperous attitude. Look at it daily so it is in your mind frequently. For Heaven's sake, avoid feeling sorry for yourself.

One of the affirmations I use is, "I have everything I need for success". I do! I have good health. I have a creative spirit in me that finds ways to make ordinary events special. You have that same advantage. The way you make something special is the way you present it. A spaghetti dinner with your family or friends becomes a special treat when you put a candle on the table and use your serving dishes and cloth napkins. Packaging is what sells the product more than what is in it.

Cosmetic companies don't sell grease. They sell creams that offer benefits. Car dealers don't sell mechanical enclosures that take you from one place to another, they sell prestige, economy, and most of all, design and appearance.

Think back to the folks who lived a hundred years ago and see how many "luxuries" you enjoy that make life easier and pleasant. One of my luxuries is my telephone which brings me close to more people I want to share my life with. Another is the supermarket which gives me a variety of foods to choose from. Also, I don't have to fuss with pulling weeds or harvesting wheat to have a loaf of bread!

There are many who go into a market who hate to shop, are thinking of how much everything costs, and feel limited because they cannot buy everything. I would rather look at it in a more positive way. I feel prosperous and they feel limited though we are in the same place. You have the same choice: to be happy or to be sad. You are the only one who can make that decision.

I have made a list of ways to feel poor. I made it in jest and hope you get a laugh at some of the ideas. When you are saving money by not spending it, think about what will make it fun instead of sad.

WAYS TO FEEL POOR

- Never have enough money with you even if you know you will need it.
- Never water your plants and never throw away a sick one; it might get well.
- Don't plant colorful flowers near your front door; after all, you are going to redo the yard when your ship comes in.
- Don't mend your old dress, just put it in the closet where you can look at it all the time and push it aside every time you want something to wear.
- Don't wash your car, never polish it, and keep the old trash from McDonald's inside. There might be a french fry you can nibble on.
- Make your friends feel sorry for you by telling them how hard it is for you to pay your share of the tab. Actually, this will save you money, because they won't ask you the next time. Then you can make them feel worse by saying, "How come you didn't ask me?"

- Before you go anywhere, ask how much everything will cost and what can you get out of paying.
- Never pick up the tab, wait until someone else offers.
- When you receive a compliment for something you have, tell how little you paid for it, and what the one you really want costs.
- Tell your family you are cutting down on their presents this year. It makes them feel great.
- Don't take a coat when it is cold. If you shiver a lot, people will feel sorry for you.
- Don't bring the hostess a gift if you are invited to dinner.
- Make sure you have a run in your hose. Maybe someone will offer to buy you some.
- Don't tell jokes on yourself or laugh; after all, if you want to look poor, you can't be happy. If you look happy, people will suspect you can afford more than you can and pressure you to spend money.
- Always give a long detailed reason why you cannot spend money. This will reinforce your attitude of being a failure.

Now for some practical ways to not spend money. Delay is one of the best tactics for avoiding an expense. Put off writing a check for cash if you can get by a little longer. One day, one week, or even one month of not spending for extras can mean paying off a bill.

When you get an increase in pay, delay adding that amount into spending for a more expensive lifestyle. Put the difference in the bank and continue to live on the income you had before.

When you have an "opportunity" to make a purchase, consider the following questions before you buy. Remember, no one makes you part with your money. You are the one who decides.

BUYER'S TEST

1. Is this what I want? Is this purchase part of my plan?

2. Why do I want it? Is there something I want more?

3. Does my decision have to be made this moment?

4. How will I feel if I don't buy it?

5. Am I buying this because I feel sorry for myself?

6. What are the results if I purchase this? How will I pay for it?

7. Is it important to discuss with my partner before taking action?

8. Is this a quality item? Is this valuable to me?

9. Will there be a cost of upkeep?

10. Am I undecided? This tells you a big NO.

AMAZING! WE ARE OFTEN VERY CREATIVE
IN MAKING OUR WANTS SEEM TO BE NEEDS!
BE AWARE OF WHAT YOU ARE DOING.

SUMMARY

1. Not spending is the easiest way to save money.

2. Some luxuries are necessary to our well-being.

3. Spending freely means not having to be concerned about the results.

4. It is important to feel prosperous while limiting expenses. List your luxuries.

5. The package is more important than the product. How you present things can give you a feeling of prosperity.

6. Ways to feel poor, the obvious reverse of what we want.

7. Delay is one way to save. Delay using additional income by living on what you had before.

8. Feeling sorry for yourself is self-destructive.

9. Take THE BUYER'S TEST to use before making a purchase.

Chapter Fourteen

SAVING MONEY BY SETTING IT ASIDE

- Saying "Yes" means saying "No" to something else.
- It is easier to save during inflation.
- Be for something, rather than against everything else.

Every time we say "Yes" to something, we are saying "No" to something else. Just as the number of things you could be doing right now is limitless, yet you are reading this book. By saying "Yes" to reading this book, you have said "No" to all the other things you could be doing. The potential is always greater than what happens.

Every time we spend money for something we have decided to not spend money on something else. We have choices. The pessimist will give attention to the limitations and the optimist will concentrate on the choice made rather than what might have been. If you are thinking about something else, you are not giving your full attention to reading. This cuts down the power of energy you give to this moment. The same thing happens when you make a decision to spend money. If you have doubts about what you are doing, you will not enjoy your choice.

Deciding to save money is a commitment only if you give a whole-hearted effort to doing so.

Believe it or not, it is easier to save in inflationary times because you are handling more money. For instance, in 1934 my parents paid 5¢ for a loaf of bread. In 1992, the cost is $1.79. It is easier to set aside part of 179 units than it is to set aside part of 5 units. Especially when the total monthly income in 1934 was $40.00 for my parents.

"Ah," I hear you say, "saving money is not profitable because it is worthless and loses value as the years go by." I can agree with you that it won't buy as much as it does today. However, anyone with cash during a time when others are having a hard time holding on to real or personal property, will be in a better position to acquire those properties at a discount price. Taking over payments on an automobile can be less costly than having bought it new 10 months before. If you spend everything you have, you will not be able to take advantage of bargains. There are always bargains. Be in a position to help someone be relieved of the problem of maintaining ownership. Save money that is readily available to you.

Investments are for long-term gain and do not qualify as liquid assets if you have to sell the investment before you have cash. Investments are for those who have a cash reserve for emergency and short-term opportunity first.

You need a reserve for yourself and your family. Life does hold surprises. No one ever planned to have an accident. If they knew they were going to have one, they wouldn't have gone there. And no one planned on having an accident with the other driver who has no insurance. Boy, aren't you glad you have enough to pay the rent while you are disabled and your income drops or stops.

Young people can possibly get by with a reserve of three months income. They have the advantage of youth by being more apt to find new employment sooner, should they lose their job. They are more apt to heal faster if they are injured. And they are more likely to have other family members who can help them.

Older (than very young) people need a six months to one year reserve. If they lose their job, they may have to wait longer to find new employment at their level; the more selective talent can mean it is harder to find the right position. (Sometimes it takes a professional or highly skilled person a year or more to find a position.) Their expenses are possibly higher and they have to consider what they will do for income when they retire. Using all their reserves can set them back further.

In order to set more money aside, a plan of spending less is needed. We talked about that in the last chapter, but here is another thought. Lunch out costs less than dinner, breakfast costs less than lunch, and breakfast at home and coffee out is still an outing. And just because you are out to dinner doesn't mean you have to order an entrée. Have soup and salad if that is what you want. Look at everything you do and evaluate how to gain the same type of pleasure with less cash outlay. Make it fun and don't feel sorry for yourself.

I heard of a woman who got her husband to agree that when she prepared a meal at home when normally they went out, he would give her the amount dinner would have cost. The money went into a fund and they took a beautiful trip through the United States visiting places they had always meant to see. She made those meals fun as she gave a special effort to have flowers on the table and to use candlelight. It became a game and they laughed all the way to the bank.

Another way to save money is to put aside what it costs to buy an item before you take delivery. A refrigerator paid for in cash costs you less than one you make payments on. You can save the amount needed, use your credit card for the purchase, pay it off within the thirty day limit with your savings, and come out ahead.

An extra part-time job can be the source of your savings. Be careful of investing in an inventory of products you have to sell in order to realize a profit. Not everyone is a salesman. If you have never sold to your friends before, you may find you have spent more than you take in, after going into direct sales. Learning to sell is an excellent experience. It is easier for the enthusiastic person than the shy person. Being totally sold on what you are selling is so important. If you believe it is the absolutely best product on the market and you yourself would not be without it, then you have a chance of making more money than if you took an hourly wage job. There are people who make $80,000 a year in direct sales. I know one personally. The caution is that most people who try this barely meet expenses.

You have heard it before and it has to be true that the best way to save money is to put it into a savings account before you pay other bills. One of my friends goes for a walk to the savings and loan close to his work every time he receives his paycheck and puts $50.00 or more in an account. This is in addition to his regular savings. Every time he walks in, the tellers kid him about making another deposit because he does not ever take out money, he just puts it in. They love him. He loves how that account grows. Just in case you think it is easy for him to set aside money, I should mention he has a beautiful wife who works hard, but does not earn an income. She stays home and cares for their seven children. If a man with a large family can do it, you can.

You need more than one savings account, but I will be happy if you start with just one if you have never saved money before. What you will want to do is have different accounts for different goals. One account will be your reserve account for the red card expenses in your COLORCODE CARD SYSTEM.

Be for something rather than against anything. For instance, I am not really against anything, I just don't like some things. There are those people who thrive on overcoming obstacles and do things "in spite of the difficulties". And then there is me and others like me who enjoy doing things because of possibilities. Life is fun for me. I feel blessed beyond words. I smile a lot. I laughingly tell my associates, "Never trust someone who smiles a lot. They may know something you don't know." What I know is that being for things lets energy flow and things happen that are productive. Should I try to be against something, I risk letting down my guard and then I lose.

For instance, if I am using willpower to lose weight, I must watch calories and think about avoiding fattening foods. It is so much easier to use my imagination to create a picture of health and slimness and to eat as if I am already slim. To be thinking about food when losing weight is to tempt myself and to desire the thing I don't need. The best way for me is to eat at mealtime only and to cancel all thought of food in between.

It is the same thing with saving money. Don't be thinking about what you are not going to buy, think about how your savings account is growing. If you have a strong belief in what you are doing, you will not be deterred from your plan.

You have a budget or plan now. Anytime you spend, that is part of your plan. (Your plan could be very loose now and what we are talking about is having a stronger plan). Having a plan of how I want to spend is stronger than just paying bills until the money is spent. I am not against spending money, I am for spending it so it brings me pleasure.

You are fortunate if you have two incomes in your family and can live on one and use the other for pleasure and savings. You are also fortunate if you have an automatic withdrawal from your checking account into your savings account. If you have an interest-bearing checking account, you are really ahead of the game. If you have a deduction from your paycheck for a savings account, then you are really clever. These are all part of your plan and they help you save money by setting it aside before you spend it.

Remember when we started this chapter and I talked about saying "Yes" to something? Say "Yes" to your savings plan. A person who has saved has the unfair advantage over those who have spent everything. HERE'S to the UNFAIR ADVANTAGE!

SUMMARY

1. Every time we say "Yes" to something, we are saying "No" to something else.

2. Deciding to save money is a commitment only if you give a whole-hearted effort to doing so.

3. It is easier to save during inflationary times.

4. Having a savings account can put you in a position to help someone be relieved of the problem of maintaining ownership. (Plus help save you money).

5. You need a reserve of three months to a year's income just for emergencies.

6. Saving money can be made into a fun project.

7. Save first before paying bills.

8. An extra job or a second income can be just for your savings.

9. Be for something rather than against anything. Be for a savings plan.

10. The UNFAIR ADVANTAGE is having cash available in your savings account.

Chapter Fifteen

SOPHISTICATED COCKTAIL PARTY CONVERSATION
OR
AVOIDING GUILT FEELINGS ABOUT WHAT YOU JUST LEARNED. . .
BUT EVERYBODY ELSE ALREADY KNEW

- No one is in the 100% tax bracket.
- Tax evasion is illegal, tax avoidance is expected.
- There will always be opportunities.

I love to talk about money! Mine or someone else's. The talk at cocktail parties about money is fascinating. You hear outrageous statements like, "It is a tax deduction for me so it didn't cost me anything". Have people really convinced themselves of that? I look closely into their eyes and they don't even flinch. What an illusion!

No one is in the 100% tax bracket. There really is no free lunch. When you spend $1,000.00 for a toy and you make it a business expense, even if you are in the high income tax bracket, you are out of pocket $500.00. That means you do not have $500.00 to reinvest in your business. I am not against spending money for your own pleasure. Love and joy are the greatest reasons for living. What I am concerned about is the self-delusion.

A word about our sponsor, the IRS. They have determined a great deal about how we spend money by encouraging spending money for business expenses that are deductible. A lot of people use the IRS as an excuse to do things that are not in line with true honesty. You feel like a fool if you overpay taxes. Tax evasion is illegal. Tax avoidance is expected and perfectly legal. To feel guilty about taking deductions that are questionable and hoping to not be audited is an uncomfortable position. A good accountant helps you get all the deductions you are entitled to, but cannot guarantee everything they suggest is going to pass the IRS test.

The prudent person will look at each expenditure for what it really is, justified as aiding increased revenues into their business or their employer's business, and decide if they want to spend the money whether it is tax deductible or not. Tax deductible is a bonus and not the only reason to spend money. Tax deductible means you get a discount.

Think about tax audits and do keep records which include your appointment book.

Tax shelters are another favorite topic of the cocktail party people. Tax shelter usually means delayed taxes rather than no taxes. Most tax shelters are very risky. That is why they are given the advantage of delaying taxes. By offering the tax advantage, more capital is put into investing in ventures that expand the gross national product figure. Venture capital is risky.

My accountant told me that if you won a million dollars at Las Vegas, paid the tax on it, and had the balance to use as you liked, you would be better off than if you find a tax shelter, avoid paying taxes, and then lose your investment.

I question the sales pitch, "You will be in a lower tax bracket at the time you retire and will pay less taxes". Who wants to be poorer when they are retired? That is when you have more time to travel and do all the things that cost money!

Here is another statement that really gets attention—"I made 70% on my money". Everybody listens. A pang of jealousy just might enter your head. It is possibly a true statement. The question that comes to my mind right away is, "How long a period of time are you talking about for your investment to pay off at 70%?". If you compare real estate investments with U.S. Treasury Bills, and are talking about percentage gain, it is not the same. You are not comparing apples to apples, as they say. The real estate gain may be over a period of two to five years. The T Bill is the rate of interest paid in one year. A seventy-percent gain over five years may be closer to 10% a year.

Sometimes what you hear is true. On the other hand, people who go to Las Vegas will tell you about how much they won and neglect to tell you what they spent to win. One more fact may change the meaning of what you hear.

I have lived in California almost all my life. For years I have heard people say, "I could have bought a lot on Balboa Island back in the forties. It cost $500.00 then". Today it could be one million dollars. Wonderful! If they did not buy it then, it was probably because they couldn't because they did not have the money. No matter how inexpensive an item is, if you don't have the money, you don't have the option. Please be polite if someone gives you this line of what they could have done. Just smile, but don't be taken in by their bragging.

It would aid you in the understanding of investments to go to an evening class at the local college and learn about financial statements, stock market jargon, real estate investments from people who are not selling you their investment.

There are places for the small investor as well as the big guys. Getting your personal finances in order is the first place to start. If you do not yet have a good system, how are you going to keep track of your invested capital? And how are you going to know if you can commit to an investment program if you don't know how much you can direct into such a plan?

People who are in business for themselves say things at cocktail parties that intrigue the person who works for someone else. It sounds so exciting to think about being president of a company. It is so impressive to hear about the big deals that these people are working on.

You can call yourself president of a one-person company that is only a part-time endeavor and be telling the truth. It sounds like I am being sarcastic, but that is not what I want you to think. Just don't be overwhelmed by what people tell you.

The truth is the small business owner is to be admired. They are risking a lot to be on their own. They seldom start out with a steady paycheck and never know exactly how much they will have next week. They have fewer benefits than the employees of bigger companies and are risking their own and their family's security with the hope of making it big. More power to them. But don't expect them to tell you the scary part at a party. They want you to think of them as successful.

There are so many businesses that go out of business before their second year is up. Nice honest people who put so much time and effort into something they believe in. It is sad as most of them are undercapitalized. They are often naive about the real costs of doing business. It is also sad that their savings disappear.

Often, because they do not want to share profits, they will not seek an investor. One hundred percent of nothing is a lot less than 50% of something. One reason they do not go to a bank before they go into business and ask for money is they really don't want anyone to know how close to the bottom of their reserves they are and how much they are counting on immediate success to pull them through.

The most touching statement I have heard is HOW COULD WE LOSE WHEN WE WERE SO SINCERE? If you are thinking about going into business, do not be afraid to get help from others who may know more than you. Working for someone else in the same business you plan to start is a great learning experience. Learning from others saves us mistakes that can be costly. Being in business for yourself is or can be really great. There are more small businesses in the USA than big companies. People who are their own bosses usually work harder than if they worked for someone else. Doing it your way is a great challenge. Struggling and worrying all the time is not much fun. Go into a new venture with as much information as possible.

SUMMARY

1. Talking about money can be fun.

2. No one is in the 100% tax bracket. Tax deductible does not mean free.

3. Tax evasion is illegal; tax avoidance is expected.

4. Tax shelters are not tax free and you can lose more than if you paid taxes.

5. The gain on investment is given in percentages usually, but be sure the percentages are started on a per year basis if you are going to compare.

6. There are lots of stories about opportunities which were missed. They will be saying those things about today's opportunities, too. If you don't have the money, you don't have the option.

7. Learn about investments from someone other than a salesperson.

8. Having a plan for daily living is necessary before getting into investments.

9. Being in business for yourself is to be admired. You are risking a lot of security if you start a new business. Get all the information possible so you don't make unnecessary mistakes.

Chapter Sixteen

BE HONEST WITH YOURSELF

The following statements and quizzes will help you learn to know yourself better and will give insight into your habits and attitudes.

PERSONAL ATTITUDES

- I spend money wisely.
- I pay attention to what needs to be done to keep a good credit rating.
- I keep records of what I spend.
- I enjoy the money I have.
- I am not fearful about the future.
- I am grateful to be able to live a good life in a pleasant environment.
- I do not obligate myself or others financially.
- I share what I have generously.
- I am open to new ideas that generate income for me.
- I am able to visualize the success of my efforts.
- I am worthy of what I have.
- I take care of what I have without being fearful or overprotective that it could be taken from me or ruined.

- My possessions do not possess me nor do I clutch tightly to my possessions.
- I accept changes in circumstances with no fear; even the difficult times are not forever.
- I believe I am meant to be joyful and loving right now, first to myself, and then to all others.

QUESTIONNAIRE

- Do you have a checking account that is more than three years old?
- How much money do you need in your wallet in order to feel comfortable?
- Are you an impulse buyer?
- Do you feel bad about how much things cost?
- Do you feel guilty about spending for yourself?
- Do you argue with your family about money?
- Are you financially embarrassed very often?
- Do you pay bills as soon as they arrive in the mail?
- Do you feel prosperous?
- Do you wait until the last minute to shop for what you want to wear to a special function?
- Are you afraid of theft or vandalism of your valuables?
- Are you concerned about being ripped off on the price you pay for some things?
- Do you hate to take things back to the store when you are dissatisfied?

- Do you think your lifestyle is comfortable?
- Do you have a special purchase in mind that you would like to afford?
- Is it difficult to say "No" to salespeople?
- Are you a good salesman when you want to sell something or convince someone else of an idea?
- Do you think you could afford another payment right now? How much seems insignificant to you?—$25 a month?—$50 a month?—$100 a month?—$200 a month?
- Do you have money left over after you pay your bills?
- Do you consider cash that you spend unimportant, or do you watch it carefully?
- Do you know how much you spend out of your wallet—in a week?—in a month?—in a year?
- What time of day do you spend the most money?
- Do you spend more money when you are with friends?
- Where do you spend more freely?—At the grocery store?—In a restaurant?—In a department store?—On a vacation?
- What percentage do you tip waiters and waitresses? Does their service to you have an influence upon how much you tip?
- How much do you put in the church collection? How much do you think your grandmother put in?—Was her income higher than yours?—Does your contribution have as much value as hers

did, taking into consideration what your contribution will pay for?

- How often do you deny yourself even if you can afford what you are considering spending?
- What are your luxuries?—Your car?—Your phone?—Your clothes?—Your home?—Vacations?
- What would you choose if you could afford any of the following:—A first class hotel?—A second most expensive hotel?—The least expensive but clean hotel?
- Would you use the services of a first class hotel?—Valet parking?—Room service?—Dry cleaning?—Barber or Beauty Shop?—Massage?—Health Club?
- Would you pay more while on vacation for the above than for the same service in your own area?
- What makes you feel good about money?-Having a credit card with lots of credit dollars available?—Being able to pay cash?—Having a savings account that grows each month?—Having extra cash in your wallet?—Buying something on time that is expensive?—Buying something at a bargain price?—Being able to buy at a premium price in elegant surroundings?
- What services do you prefer to pay for rather than do yourself?—Hair grooming?—Car wash?—Window cleaning?—Gardening?—Housecleaning?—Secretarial services?—Other?

- How many hours do you need to work in order to generate the money needed to pay for each of the above?
- If you are living on the interest of your investments, how much time does it take to accumulate the money for the above?
- Can you make more money with your time if you hire services instead of doing the above yourself?
- Have you had more than three traffic tickets for speeding in your life?
- When did you last buy something that cost a lot of money? What was it?
- How did you feel about how you would pay for it?
- Were you sure you would be able to meet the payments? Or did you just hope you would be able to make them?
- Do you resent it when your credit is denied?
- Whose fault is it if the payments are too much for you?—The salesman?—The lender?—Your other bills?—The raise in rent or other unexpected expenses?—Some other purchase after you had this payment to make?—A drop in your income?
- What length of time seems long to you for making payments?

  —Six months?

  —One year?

  —Three years?

  —Five years?

  —Thirty years?

- What makes a bargain?
  —Price?

  —Need?

  —Want?

  —Availability?

  —Something others have that you want also?
- Do you have a reserve of cash for emergencies?
- Do you have health insurance?
- Do you have enough life insurance to cover the debts you owe?
- Do you have a will?
- How much money will you have to live on after you retire?
- Do you have a system of paying bills?
- Do you have reserve cash to cover unexpected expenditures such as major car repairs?
- How many checks do you write each month?
- How many bills do you receive in the mail each month?
- Have you had notices that your payment is late on any of your routine bills?
- Have you ever had one of your checks bounce? What was the reason?
- Do you check your bank statement?
- Do you pay your credit card bills in total each month, or do you make payments?
- Have you taken a vacation during the last year?

- Did you have enough money to pay for the vacation before you went?
- Do you spend all your income?
- Do you have a retirement fund set aside?
- Do you have more than one bank checking account?
- Do you have at least one savings account?
- Do you know the people at your bank by name? Do they know you?
- Do you feel comfortable when you write every check, knowing you have enough money to cover it?
- Do you have big-company benefits such as health insurance?

Chapter Seventeen

THE UNFAIR ADVANTAGE

- Dreams are goals not yet complete.
- You deserve good fortune.
- Cash is the unfair advantage.

Most of us want the unfair advantage. I know I do. To be more wealthy, to have more of what I want, to be in a position of having solved most of my problems and the confidence that I can solve the future ones as they come along, to be free of negative concerns, and to have a more joyous lifestyle. I want to keep my good health and my good friends. And I want to see my family prosper as much or more than I. Those are dreams. Dreams are also called hopes and aspirations. In order to dream, our basic needs have to be met first. The COLORCODE CARD SYSTEM is helping me now to get ready for all those good things.

Dreams are goals not yet complete. Dreams can come true only if you believe the goal is possible, if you can visualize yourself really doing what you want. If you can see and feel how it will be, then you are halfway there. Instead of waiting to see what will happen, make some things happen. Just adjusting and coping is only surviving.

The majority of people in the world are worried and frightened. People who have a positive attitude and a strong self esteem—knowing they deserve all the good things that they have—have a tremendous advantage! It seems as if it is an *unfair advantage* to those who do not understand. My goal in writing this book was to share attitudes of success, to build your self-esteem, and to give you tools for creating a better world for yourself. If you make the effort to utilize the information, you will be relieved of much unnecessary stress. The cup is half empty to the pessimist and half full to the optimist, but I wish for you a cup that is full and overflowing with prosperity. Why be limited or fearful? Why not be happy? It is a choice each of us makes. The world will gain as we gain. Age has nothing to do with it. Growth into becoming a more responsible person brings excitement rather than drama into our lives.

People who have a positive attitude and strong self-esteem— knowing they deserve all the good things that the possess—have a tremendous advantage!

You deserve to be successful. Know you are unique and worthy. Act like you are worthy.

For most of my life, I had misunderstood what the word humble meant. I thought that humble was the opposite of confident. Don't ask me where I got the idea, but it was part of my thinking and I have always striven toward all the things that give me confidence. It is only recently that I have given a different meaning to humble. Humble to me now means being open. Open to learning new ways to do things, and most of all, new ways to think about myself and others.

You can be humble and still have dignity. In fact, you gain more dignity. You can be humble and have strong convictions. Things that are true for you. But that is the key—they are good for you, but may not be what someone else thinks is good for them. Humble folk let others be what they are.

You can be humble and wealthy. There is no conflict there. A wealthy person can be open and kind, and can be generous in how he thinks about others, accepting others as they are, as well as be generous with his wealth.

Dream your dream. Your dream will not hurt anyone. When your dream comes true, you will be stronger to help someone else. The rich person who brings all his poverty thinking into his new wealth, does not think he deserves his wealth so he is sure others will try to take it from him. To become wealthy does not mean you cannot be happy. Being poor does not mean you will be happier than if you became rich. The people who say rich people are not happy are usually people who want to be richer, but can't see it becoming a reality. Sour grapes, I think.

The unfair advantage is knowing you deserve, knowing what you want, and knowing how to get there. The unfair advantage in today's world is having cash and a good credit rating. This book has been written for the purpose of giving you the unfair advantage of knowing how to get to a position of having expenses stay below income, and to build your reserves.

Goals need to be so clear they are simple. Goals that are simple focus energy into one accomplishment. Simple does not mean easy to the point of "no effort".

Goals need to be so satisfying that you become excited about them. The effort will flow if you are enthused.

Goals need to be obtainable. You can always make your next goal bigger, but your first goal needs to show evidence of progress soon. Start with short-term goals. Your first may be only the project of getting organized. When that is done, then setting up the COLORCODE CARD SYSTEM. When that is done, work out the CASH FLOW CHART. The next might be opening a savings account. You do not have to do everything at one time.

Goals need to have deadlines. If there were no end to the time you had to make something happen, it would never happen. Set a time for your first goal to be complete. Then a time for your second goal to be done. Proceed until you are satisfied. You are the one whom you are satisfying. The feeling of accomplishment is the greatest motivation for wanting the feeling again and again. Procrastination takes away such a good feeling.

The unfair advantage is unfair only to those who do not understand. The unfair advantage is earned. Knowledge is the real advantage. Be glad you know how to make your dreams come true.

HERE'S TO THE UNFAIR ADVANTAGE!

SUMMARY

1. Most of us want the unfair advantage.

2. Dreams are goals not yet complete.

3. You can know you deserve good fortune.

4. Your dream will not hurt anyone.

5. The unfair advantage is knowing what you want and knowing how to get there.

6. The unfair advantage is cash and a good credit rating.

7. Goals need to be clear.

8. Goals need to be satisfying.

9. Goals need to be obtainable. You can see they are possible.

10. Goals need to have deadlines. Each step towards a goal becomes a goal of itself.

11. The unfair advantage is unfair only to those who do not understand.

12. Knowledge is the real advantage.

AFTERWORD
(As Compared to Foreword)

A TOAST TO THE UNFAIR ADVANTAGE

Here's to the unfair advantage———
　　May you run out of month before you run
　　out of money!

Here's to the unfair advantage———
　　May your wallet be fat and your body slim!

Here's to the unfair advantage———
　　May you live long and your money longer!

Here's to the unfair advantage———
　　May you glisten with diamonds, radiate
　　confidence, and lend money to your banker!

A toast to the unfair advantage———
　　May your choices in life be "Which one?"
　　rather than "How can I?"

Here's to the unfair advantage———
　　May you be financially independent of your
　　children———tell them to get rich!

Here's to the unfair advantage———
　　May you be so organized your tax man calls
　　you for an appointment!

KIT FOR COLOR CODE CARD SYSTEM
AND CASH FLOW CHART

You can get started right away!

On the following pages are suggested forms for your Color Code Card System. Copy them by hand or photocopy them onto your colored cards. Read them carefully and change what is not appropriate for your needs. You will probably need more than we have provided if you have a lot of bills to pay.

It is important to get started - Don't delay - Do it NOW!

MAILING LIST

If you want to get on our mailing list for future updates and kits, please send your name and address to:

> **Beverlee Kelley**
> **Griffin Publishing**
> **544 W. Colorado Street**
> **Glendale, CA 91204**

Name: _____

Address: _____

City, St. & Zip: _____

SAVINGS ACCOUNT

Bank Name _____

Address _____

City, State Zip _____

Account Info Phone # _____

Account # _____

Manager: _____

Pay on _____ day of the Month

Amount $ _____

12 Months Goal $ _____

Date	Check #	Amount	Balance

GREEN CARD

FOR ASSETS SUCH AS SAVING, MORTGAGE, IRAS, ETC.

SAVINGS ACCOUNT

Bank Name_____

Address _____

City, State Zip _____

Account Info Phone # _____

Account # _____

Manager: _____

Pay on ____ day of the Month

Amount $ _____

12 Months Goal $ _____

Date	Check #	Amount	Balance

GREEN CARD

FOR ASSETS SUCH AS SAVING, MORTGAGE, IRAS, ETC.

Company _____
Address _____
City, State Zip _____

Billing Info Phone # _____
Emergency Phone # _____

Day of the Month _____
12 Months $ _____

Date	Check #	Amount	Year to Date

WHITE CARDS

FOR UTILITIES, TELEPHONE, PAID UP CREDIT CARDS, ETC.

Company _____
Address _____
City, State Zip _____

Billing Info Phone # _____
Emergency Phone # _____

Day of the Month _____
12 Months $ _____

Date	Check #	Amount	Year to Date

WHITE CARDS

FOR UTILITIES, TELEPHONE, PAID UP CREDIT CARDS, ETC.

LOAN _____   Account Info Phone # _____   Day of the Month _____
Bank Name _____   Account # _____ $ _____
Address _____   Term ___ years   12 Months $ _____
City, State Zip _____   Amount of Loan $ _____

Date	Check #	Amount	Principal	Interest	Balance Due

BLUE CARDS
FOR DEBTS SUCH AS CREDIT CARD BALANCES, LOANS, ETC.

LOAN _____   Account Info Phone # _____   Day of the Month _____
Bank Name _____   Account # _____ $ _____
Address _____   Term ___ years   12 Months $ _____
City, State Zip _____ Amount of Loan $ _____

Date	Check #	Amount	Principal	Interest	Balance Due

BLUE CARDS
FOR DEBTS SUCH AS CREDIT CARD BALANCES, LOANS, ETC.

Purpose _____

$_____ a week
12 months $_____

Date	Check #	Amount	Total to Date

YELLOW CARDS

FOR PLEASURABLE THINGS SUCH AS VACATIONS, CLOTHES, ALLOWANCE, HOBBIES, ETC.

Purpose _____

$ _____ a week
12 months $ _____

Date	Check #	Amount	Total to Date

YELLOW CARDS
FOR PLEASURABLE THINGS SUCH AS VACATIONS, CLOTHES, ALLOWANCE, HOBBIES, ETC.

SAVINGS ACCOUNT

Account Info Phone # _____

Day of the Month _____

Bank Name _____

Account # _____

Amount $ _____

Address _____

Manager: _____

12 Months Goal $ _____

City, State Zip _____

Date	Check #	Amount	Balance

RED CARDS
FOR HOLIDAYS, BIRTHDAYS, AUTO INSURANCE AND OTHER PERIODIC EXPENSES

SAVINGS ACCOUNT

Bank Name _____

Address _____

City, State Zip _____

Account Info Phone # _____

Account # _____

Manager: _____

Day of the Month _____

Amount $ _____

12 Months Goal $ _____

Date	Check #	Amount	Balance

RED CARDS

FOR HOLIDAYS, BIRTHDAYS, AUTO INSURANCE AND OTHER PERIODIC EXPENSES

Look for all these and other fine Griffin Books
at your favorite bookstore or write to:
GRIFFIN PUBLISHING

(Please Print)   Date _____

Name _____

Address _____

City _____ State _____ Zip _____

Phone (_____) _____

KANTAR ON BRIDGE

Edward B. Kantar is a world-renowned author on bridge, and winner
of many national and international tournaments.

The books available here are not meant for beginners, nor are they
aimed at experts. They are directed at players somewhere between
these extremes who would like to improve their game substantially.
Could this be you?

	PRICE	QTY.	AMOUNT
A New Approach to Play and Defense	$10.95		
A Treasury of Bridge Bidding Tips	$10.95		
A Treasury of Bridge Playing Tips	$10.95		
	Sub-total		
	CA res. add 8.25%		
	Shipping		
	TOTAL		

Shipping: 1st book, $1.50
2nd book, $1.00 each

Check type of payment:

____ Check or money order enclosed

____ Visa   ____ Mastercard

Acct. # _____

Exp. Date _____

Signature _____

Send order to:
**Griffin Publishing
544 W. Colorado St.
Glendale, CA 91204**
Or call to order:
**1-800-423-5789 CA
1-800-826-4849 USA**